An Unauthorized Guide to

Godzilla
Collectibles

Sean Linkenback

Schiffer Publishing Ltd

4880 Lower Valley Road, Atglen, PA 19310

Copyright © 1998 by Sean Linkenback
Library of Congress Catalog Card Number: 98-84391

Designed by Blair Loughrey
Typeset in *Van Dijk/Zurich BT*

ISBN: 0-7643-0544-1
Printed in China
1 2 3 4

Published by Schiffer Publishing Ltd.
4880 Lower Valley Road
Atglen, PA 19310
Phone: (610) 593-1777; Fax: (610) 593-2002
E-mail: Schifferbk@aol.com
Please write for a free catalog.
This book may be purchased from the publisher.
Please include $3.95 for shipping.

In Europe, Schiffer books are distributed by
Bushwood Books
6 Marksbury Avenue
Kew Gardens
Surrey TW9 4JF England
Phone: 44 (0) 181 392-8585; Fax: 44 (0) 181 392-9876
E-mail: Bushwdea.aol.com

Please try your bookstore first.

We are interested in hearing from authors
with book ideas on related subjects.

Contents

Acknowledgments

A volume of this magnitude certainly could not have been accomplished without the help of several people, to whom I am very grateful. At the top of any list of course would have to be my wife Jennie, who not only put up with me working all hours of the night, and allowed many things to come into our collection "for the sake of the book," but who also photographed everything in the book. Next would be Ed Godziszewski, without whom, I don't think I would have half of the information that I do now. I would also like to thank both the dealers who helped out with the pricing averages for the book and the other collectors who gave advice and input: Scott Horton, Chris Beard, Keith Contarino, Jim Cironella, John Chruscinski, Greg Cordero, Clay Croker, Jerry Jacobs, Shane Morton, Fabian Medina, J.D. Lees, Sunny Prowett, Ken Schacter, and Ken Shain. And, of course, special thanks to my friends and helpers in Japan, most notably Norihiko Asao, Jun Hyodo, Masahiro & Canico Kizawa, Kyoko Morizumi, and Sasano.

Foreword

"Could you write something about how you put your collection together?" was the question. While the answer was an enthusiastic yes, as I now sit in the 9' x 11' room which serves as home to what I can display from over 32 years of collecting, the enormity of the task really sets in. The phrase which so often comes to my mind—whenever asked how much I have or how much did I spend over the years of collecting—is "more than is wise to admit to."

Though I collect several different subjects, without question Godzilla/Japanese science fiction has been and will always be my favorite. No doubt I feel like many collectors these days ... as display space becomes increasingly scarce, one constantly fights to squeeze in just one more item, making the display ever more dense. And considering that the undisplayed items are stored directly below in our crawl space, the total must surely strain the capacity of the earth's crust to withstand such a concentrated mass. So, just how did this all come to be? I must admit to having had the luxury of time on my side, starting over 25 years ago when today's vintage items were far less expensive. And no less valuable has been establishing several friendships which worked to our mutual collecting benefit—especially important when one has modest financial resources, limited access to collectibles, and is unable to play ball in the big money collectors market.

Before describing how I managed to assemble my collection, it seems appropriate to ask what is it that I collect and why? I must confess to something that might make most collectors cringe ... I just collect what I like and can reasonably afford, and even if it is a "rare" or "famous" item, if I don't like it I will likely pass on it. Mind you, there isn't much about Godzilla that I don't like, but even though they are among the rarest and most sought after, one could not give me a Marusan Minya doll or an Mattel Godzilla—so ugly that I cannot stand them. But I will search high and low for a stinky ¥100 capsule monster that I need to complete a set of caricature rubber monsters or blow $10 on a still of Nick Adams and Kumi Mizuno from Monster Zero. And I do not view much of what I collect as any kind of investment ... I get what I like, and

I get it because I want to keep it. The only time I plan to get rid of something (except perhaps in a trade) is when I die. And, to an extent, I like to enjoy what I have. So, much to the horror of purists, while I won't use my Godzilla shampoo or drink my Godzilla Cola, I do actually open and BUILD model kits, I will remove a tag from a vinyl doll because I want to look at the figure without the stupid tag covering half of it (but at least I always retain the packaging), I open candy boxes to see and display the monster figures hidden inside, and I have even played my LPs.

How did it all start? The beginning goes back to the summer of 1963 when *King Kong vs. Godzilla* was released in this country. As an impressionable 9-year old dinosaur lover, when I saw the trailer for this film, I immediately felt something special—this was the greatest dinosaur ever! I eagerly attended the film the next week (the only one of my friends rooting for Godzilla) as well as the big creature's subsequent theatrical releases. Perhaps, like many collectors of my age, my first Godzilla item was Aurora's plastic Godzilla kit, with its exciting box art—lightning bolt flashing in the background and blood on Godzilla's green arms. Never mind that Godzilla was not actually green nor ever shed human blood on screen ... those were details unimportant to an excited kid who never spent a sum as high as $1.29 in his life to that time (don't laugh—this shows just how different life was in the 1960s).

Despite my repeated and fervent requests, I never did convince my parents to part with $3.49 for Ideal's Godzilla Game which was also released at that time, and to this day it remains one of the saddest holes in my collection. Aside from some newspaper clippings of movie ads and an issue or two of Famous Monsters, these comprised the sum total of my "collection" for almost 10 years. Add to that a few of Ken Films' black & white 8mm reels, and I thought I had gotten everything available.

The big breakthrough in my Godzilla collecting came in the mid-1970s. Around that time I found a comic shop in the area which carried various magazines including *Film Collectors World*. On a whim I picked up an issue, only to discover that all the posters and stills which I drooled over in the theaters could actually be bought! I remember well that a place called *The Cinema Attic* was the source of my first posters and lobby cards—1-sheets on *Ghidrah* and *Destroy All Monsters* for $5 each, a *King Kong vs. Godzilla* lobby set for $8, various 8 x 10 stills, and a then budget-busting $20 for a 3-sheet poster of the original *Godzilla*. As I opened the envelope and found inside what I previously thought had been completely unattainable, that first rush of excitement was unforgettable. In the following months I eagerly scoured the ads in *Film Collectors' World* and *Cinema Attic* catalogs, finding odds and ends, even a few European pieces. Another big break came when I attended Star Trek '75 in Chicago, my first introduction to a convention dealers room. There I found several other items at reasonable prices, such as a *Godzilla vs. The Thing* 3-sheet for $5, a wealth of stills, and even 16mm trailers. With prices generally reasonable, I was able to amass the majority of my American poster/still/lobby card collection at that time. But at that time, items from Japan seemed all but an impossibility.

All that changed around 1975 when *Famous Monsters* did their now-coveted All Japanese Monster Issue, #114. For one, it provided me with information (and misinformation as well) and pictures of several Godzilla films about which I had never heard. More importantly, however, it contained an ad for a fan magazine called *Japanese Fantasy Film Journal* published by Greg Shoemaker in Ohio. I wrote as quickly as I could and was able to buy 3 issues—#6, 10, and 11. Not only had I found that indeed there was a lot of good information out there on Japanese films, but there were also a lot of other people interested in Godzilla besides me. Through *JFFJ*, I eventually made contact with several local fans who introduced me to a whole world of information about Japanese monsters and collectibles which I never knew existed. Through their kindness, I was introduced to other fans in the US and Canada, several of whom I was able to trade with or buy items from. They also gave me my first contact in Japan. From that moment, things began to happen rapidly.

The timing of my contact with a Japanese friend was quite fortuitous. While unable to track down vintage Japanese toys, he was able to provide me with my first two Japanese 1-sheets (reissues of Ghidrah and Sea Monster) and one of the rarest of Japanese books, *The Films of Eiji Tsuburaya*. Prior to this time, Toho had sparsely merchandised their properties, with a scant few books and only the Marusan/Bullmark toy line to show for their efforts. But now Toho saw a resurgence in interest in monsters and they started to aggressively merchandise their films again, leading to new toy lines from Popy/Bandai and a host of new books. The path to it all was provided by my Japanese friend. This was perhaps the most enjoyable time that I experienced in collecting ... those first steps into previously unknown worlds were exhilarating. Books like *Fantastic Collection #5—Godzilla* and *Complete Collection of Godzilla* published incredible photos never seen previously. Popy's roaring Jumbosaurus figure was the first toy of its size as well as the first to issue an authentic roar. Those were days when the mailman's arrival was eagerly anticipated, hoping that something in the day's delivery might bear that friendly postmark from Japan. While I still greatly enjoy getting new items today (and in many ways today's merchandise is of better quality), the quantity available is now huge and the availability (even in the US) is far greater. The sense of discovery and of attaining the impossible-to-get that prevailed in the late 1970s seldom happens these days.

The next incremental leap in collecting came when I finally decided to visit Japan in 1979. While there were actually just a few items available in Japanese stores at that time, I was able to expand my network of friends in Japan and, consequently, my access to future items. Although short-lived, I did make a contact with someone who had access to a large selection of vintage posters and paid/traded what at the time seemed exorbitant prices for old posters (roughly $50 each for some 1960s titles). But in moments of fiscal irresponsibility (and what in retrospect seems good judgment along the lines of "you may never have this chance again"), I went ahead and paid the ransom. Since poster shops in Japan are few and far between (the first I ever found in Japan would appear in 1990), it seemed the only way to go.

I returned to Japan in 1982 to attend a convention in Tokyo and happened across one dealer with a stack of old posters including Toho titles, almost all of which disappeared within 15 minutes of appearing on the table. While I only found a couple titles that I needed, a nearby dealer also had what I still consider to be the prize piece of my collection, an original Japanese poster of my favorite film, *Godzilla vs. The Thing*. This convention also marked the introduction of garage kits, in this case 50cm tall resin kits of Godzilla (vs. the Thing) and Baragon. Both were cast in a sticky and somewhat brittle petroleum-based resin that had a strong odor to it. These were really limited edition prototypes, the forerunners of garage kits, with many to follow in years to come. Only by being in the right place at the right time was I able to obtain them.

Being where I needed to be when I needed to be there also explains my good fortune in obtaining several other limited or unreleased garage kits. Developing a good relationship with the friendly folks at Kaiyodo (an Osaka-based garage kit manufacturer), I had the chance to obtain a rare 40cm solid-resin Moth-Godzi and 30cm resin Alpha submarine (*Latitude Zero*), a miniature Hedorah, and a few others. And in the early days of garage kits, when the exchange rate was still a more purchase-friendly ¥260/$, I was also able to afford several large scale resin kits before resin prices escalated into the stratosphere, causing vinyl kits to take over. These solid resin kits included Volks' 1/150 King Ghidora, Rodan, Gigan, and Moth-Godzi; Inoue Arts' diorama of Kin-Godzi destroying a NATO base and Mothra dragging Godzilla by the tail; and Inoue Arts' 1/150 MechaGodzilla 2.

Godzilla started to become big business, and certainly Toho had an all-too-willing customer in myself, despite the dwindling value of the dollar against the yen. While I still eagerly snap up most of today's merchandise (either through friends in Japan or during business trips), much of which makes older items pale in comparison, that special feeling I had in previous years seldom resurfaces. Most items (though not all) are simply far easier to obtain. Even US outlets exist for a vast number of items, including the once all-but-impossible to find theater posters, if one has the resources to pay their asking prices. Perhaps the thrill of the hunt is gone to some extent, but the hunt continues today, strong as ever.

So as I look back at the last 25 years of collecting, I come to realize that a combination of a lot of good luck and the help of many friends, both at home and abroad, are largely responsible for what I have been able to put together. While every collector has their own goals and reasons for collecting, I look upon all this and have no trouble coming up with my motivation ... I love monsters and especially the greatest one of all.

Part of the joy in collecting is not only in the thrill of the hunt, but also in the pleasure of both being

The last real breakthrough which I had in collecting was in Japanese stills and lobby cards. These without exception have been, and remain to this day, the toughest items to come by. Toho keeps especially tight control over them. Very few make their way to the collectors market. My collection of Japanese stills mainly came as presents received from Japanese friends (who knows how they got them) or in trades with other fans. However, I found I could also obtain a few stills and a few sets of lobby cards from a collectors store in Tokyo called CineHouse that my Japanese friend discovered in 1992. While at that time this was a virtual paradise for older materials (if you could afford them), unfortunately since 1995 their stock has been depleted to the point that now the shop owner hardly has any remaining Toho items for sale, save a few current posters.

As the Godzilla films of the 1990s were released, Toho found its licensing sense and started authorizing scores of books, toys, and audio/video items.

able to share the results of the hunt with others and in reciprocating by helping someone else find that special item they want. There is a lot of satisfaction in that, and now my enthusiasm has even rubbed off a bit on my children as they grow up (ohh, the space ...). I can't fathom the thinking of collectors who need to be the only one to have an item. To enjoy an item less because someone else also has one seems silly, and indeed these folks seldom seem happy.

What does the future hold? To quote the motto of the family crest of James Bond, "The world is not enough" ("Good motto, eh?" says one character). I suppose most die-hard collectors feel that way. Given the proliferation of today's merchandise combined with the never-ending search for newly discovered old items, to have all that is available in the Godzilla collecting world is a goal which none of us is ever likely to achieve. But we will never stop trying ...

— Alan Smithee

Introduction

This reference and price guide is by far the most comprehensive list of Godzilla memorabilia assembled to date, in any language. We know that many people collect only toys, or only posters, or only books, CD's, or whatever. This book will attempt to be a reference for all types of collectors.

While every collector has his or her own unique way of arranging a collection or keeping an inventory of items, we have attempted to list everything in this book in well defined categories. Together with a comprehensive table of contents, the reader should be able to easily locate any item in this book. In addition, we have created a numbering code for each item, so that this book can act as your Godzilla collectibles reference bible. Each item has been assigned its own letter/number code and all pictures in this book correspond with that code. The first two letters represent the item's group code and the numbers are its unique ID number. We have also left many unused numbers, to allow for future items that we may not yet be aware of. This should allow for world-wide ease of use, as collectors around the globe will be able to exactly identify what it is they are talking about.

Collectors and dealers are free to use the codes as they see fit to describe any items they are buying, selling, or trading. However, use of these codes for purposes other than buying, selling, and/or trading material will have to be first cleared with the publisher (this includes checklists, independent updates, or any number of other unauthorized uses).

We have tried not to list any unauthorized material in this book, as there are frequently foreign "knockoff's" of many of the licensed toys and other items produced. These are not authorized by Toho Productions and are usually not of the quality associated with licensed items. Because of this, their desirability to a collector is very limited. The only exceptions to this rule are the three major American fanzines (*Japanese Fantasy Film Journal*, *Japanese Giants*, and *G-Fan*), because of their historical importance and the groundbreaking role they have provided in uniting fans.

We have made every attempt to make this book as complete as possible. However, due to the scope and size of a project like this, the fact that nothing like it has

ever been attempted before, and the limitations on time and space, there will be some omissions and possibly some errors in this edition. We encourage you to notify us with any items that you may have that are not listed, or any corrections you might have to the current listings, so that the next edition of our guide can be even better and more accurate. Please include a photo of the item if possible, as well as a complete description including height, length, color, and any other pertinent information to the address below.

Manufacturers—we would like to hear from you. Please send any brochures, product samples or relevant information to our address below, so that we may include you in future editions.

Send all letters to:
Godzilla Price Guide Update
P.O. Box 921185
Norcross, GA 30010-7185

About The Values Listed In This Guide

Even though many collectors will enjoy this book just for the incredible variety of merchandise listed (even after getting upset when finding out there is so much more than they ever dreamed), we realize that the majority of collectors and dealers buy a book like this for the pricing data inside. So we would like to take a moment to explain how prices are determined in this volume.

All values listed in this reference guide were gathered from dealers' lists, ads in magazines, convention sales, and by contact with dealers and collectors from across the world (with particular attention paid to the United States). What we have done is attempt to give a realistic average between the lowest and highest observed selling price of a particular item. All values are current market values of items just prior to the guide's publication, and reflect previous sales from this past year. We are not fortune tellers. We are not trying to list what items will be selling for in the coming year. Rather we are providing an average of what these items were bringing. Many prices will stay at this level throughout the year, but the collector is advised to keep on top of what is happening in the market by reading the fanzines,

Alan's (and most everybody's in the United States) first exposure to Godzilla-The Aurora model kit.

looking at dealer catalogs, and by attending conventions. We have gone from a time of no Godzilla theme conventions a few years ago to three major conventions held in 1997.

Also please note, several of the rarest items seldom come up for sale in any given year (especially in mint condition or mint in package for some of the toys). This can make it very difficult to arrive at a market value for these items. Such items are noted with an asterisk (*) in the listings. The author is very interested in knowing of any actual sale or discovery of previously unknown examples of these items. If you can be of assistance in this area, please write or call us.

Expect prices to vary from region to region. Prices tend to be higher on the East and West coasts, and lower in the central parts of the country. Also expect prices to vary by condition. Items in brand new condition will sell at the higher end of the price range, while items in lesser condition will, of course, sell at the lower end of the price range. Prices listed are what collectors (not dealers) would probably pay for an item. As always, the true value of an item is what you are willing to pay, not some value listed in a price guide. Prices can go up or down, so check carefully and be sure you are happy with the price you are going to pay for an item before it is too late.

All prices listed in this volume are in U.S. currency and are for your reference only. We did consider listing approximate values in Japanese Yen, but quickly

dropped the idea. For your reference, some items do have their original Japanese Yen selling price listed. This book is not a price list, although some dealers may base their prices on the values in it. Dealers usually can only pay a fraction of the price guide value of an item, depending on the amount of investment required and the quality of the material being offered. Percentages paid will usually vary from 20 to 70 percent of the guide value of an item, depending on how long the dealer thinks it will take to sell that particular item. Remember, most dealers must not only pay for your item, but also for travel, ads, phone calls, mailings, and rent ... and then hope to still make a profit for themselves in the final sale price. Not all items are in equal demand and many times a dealer will carry an item for years before finding a buyer.

One note on the Bandai vinyl's section: all prices are figured to be including the tags (or in certain instances, boxes), that come with the figures. Tags do not have to be attached for a figure to be in mint condition (most office supply stores sell machines that can re-attach the tags), but they must be present. On figures without tags, typically deduct 10-20% off the price of the figure.

A final note: MIB stands for **M**int **i**n **B**ox, while MIP means **M**int **i**n **P**ackage.

Collecting Godzilla

Chapter 1

How To Start Collecting

Starting a collection is easy enough. In fact, just buying this book can be the start of your collection. Most people will start by heading down to their local toy or book store and buying whatever items might be on the shelves. More and more Godzilla related merchandise is being released in this country and a collector could keep his or her hands full just trying to track down all the domestically produced items. Most end up frequenting several stores, just to make sure they haven't missed anything. Many advanced collectors purchase more than one of the same item, either to keep one mint in the package, to have an extra to trade with friends, or possibly to put away for resale at a future date. Of course, speculation can be a gamble, but unless collecting habits change greatly over the next few years, the value of certain Godzilla collectibles should continue to greatly appreciate. Eventually, the collector will want to start adding Japanese produced items to their collection. That begins the next step in the collector's evolution.

Where To Buy And Sell

Many collectors who are purchasing this book are also eager to find new sources of material to add to their collections or have material they wish to sell. Probably the best way to do this is to attend one of the Godzilla theme conventions listed below. If you can not attend one of the conventions, we would recommend contacting dealers and publishers. Ask for sample copies of magazines and choose a dealer listed in their pages to work with. If you are an inexperienced collector, you are encouraged to contact as many dealers as you can and compare prices before buying anything. Always place a small order the first time. That way, with a minimal investment, you can be sure that you are happy with the material you receive, with the promptness of delivery, and you can also make sure the dealer will take any returns on material you are not happy with. Remember, never send cash through the mail. For your protection, always send money orders or checks, or deal with retailers who take credit card orders.

See the Resources appendix for listings of conventions, dealers, and publications.

Although the first Godzilla movie appeared on the screens in 1954, collecting Godzilla did not really begin until at least ten years later, as that is when the toys started to appear in great numbers. Interestingly enough, even though the Japanese have produced the greatest variety and the nicest looking monster toys, it was actually the Americans who got the ball rolling.

Godzilla Movies ... A Review

Japanese Title/Year of Release	American Title/Year of Release
Gojira/1954	Godzilla, King of the Monsters/1956
Gojira no Gykushu/1955	Gigantis, the Fire Monster aka: Godzilla Raids Again/1959
Kingu Kongu tai Gojira/1962	King Kong vs. Godzilla/1963
Mosura tai Gojira/1964	Godzilla vs. the Thing aka: Godzilla vs. Mothra/1964
San Daikaiju-Chikyu Saidai No 1965 Kessen/1964	Ghidrah, the Three Headed Monster/
Kaiju Daisenso Astro-	Monster Zero aka: Invasion of the Monster/1970
Gojira, Ebirah, Mosura-Great Duel in the Ebirah, South Seas/1966	Godzilla vs. the Sea Monster aka: Horror of the Deep/1968
Kaiju Shima No Kessen-Gojira No Musuko/1967	Son of Godzilla/1968
Kaiju Soshingeki/1968	Destroy All Monsters/1969
Gojira, Minira, Gabara-Oru Kaiju Daishingeki/1969	Godzilla's Revenge/1969
Gojira tai Hedorah/1971	Godzilla vs. the Smog Monster/1972
Chikyu Kogeki Meirei-Gojira tai Gaigan Godzilla	Godzilla on Monster Island aka: vs. Gigan/1978
Gojira tai Megaro/1973	Godzilla vs. Megalon/1976
Gojira tai MekaGojira/1974	Godzilla vs. the Cosmic Monster aka: Godzilla vs. the Bionic Monster aka: Godzilla vs. MechaGodzilla/1977
MekaGojira No Gyakushu/1975	Terror of Godzilla aka: Terror of MechaGodzilla/1978
Gojira/1984	Godzilla 1985/1985
Gojira tai Biorante/1989	Godzilla vs. Biollante/1992
Gojira tai Kingu Gidora/1991	Godzilla vs. King Ghidora/unreleased
Gojira tai Mosura/1992	Godzilla vs. Mothra/unreleased
Gojira tai MekaGojira/1993	Godzilla vs. MechaGodzilla/unreleased
Gojira tai SupesuGojira/1994	Godzilla vs. SpaceGodzilla/unreleased
Gojira tai Desutoroia/1995	Godzilla vs. Destroyer/unreleased

The first licensed toy was actually a gun and target game released at the time the film *Godzilla Raids Again* was shown in Japan in 1955. This was to be the only licensed item for the next eight years. It was not until 1963, when Ideal made a Godzilla game to go along with their King Kong game, that anyone got a glimpse of what a marketing monster (pun intended) Godzilla was to become. These two games capitalized on the success of the *King Kong vs. Godzilla* movie released that year and on the two monsters in general. The movie *King Kong* was re-released to a new generation in 1956, the same year that the first Godzilla movie hit American shores. Fueled by these movies (along with a slew of others to hit the screens, as well as the emergence of *Famous Monsters of Filmland* magazine), the monster boom was on.

The second item to be released was the legendary Aurora Models' Godzilla kit in 1964. Aurora had already released a popular line of 'human sized' monster kits and had decided to release kits of the two most popular 'giant sized' monsters, King Kong and Godzilla. They sold fantastically well, even at the more expensive price of $1.29 (most other Aurora kits were priced at .98 cents).

The popularity and success of Godzilla did not go unnoticed back in Japan. The Marusan Company, makers of a wide variety of children's toys in Japan, reasoned that if a Godzilla model did so well in the States, that they could do even better with one overseas. They took the Aurora design and simplified it, gave it the "cartoony" appearance so popular in Japanese comics to appeal to children, and released it as a model kit.

This was only moderately successful in the first two years of release. It was not until 1966 when monsters and science fiction in general was booming in popularity, that Marusan decided that perhaps they should look at a well developed line of monster toys and models for children. It was at this time that the UltraQ series was released to TV, Gamera started his string of popular movies, and Godzilla was becoming more firmly entrenched as a hero rather than a protagonist.

Marusan responded by releasing several new items. For the first time, they released vinyl versions of popular monsters aimed at the children's market. For the Godzilla line this was to include Godzilla, Mothra and Ebirah from the just released *Godzilla vs. the Sea Monster*. Several monsters were also released in vinyl versions from the UltraQ series, Gamera from the new Gamera movie, DaiMajin from the movie of the same name, and Baragon from the popular *Frankenstein Con-*

quers the World. Additional releases included several high end toys such as plastic wire control kits for Baragon and Ebirah, as well as tin toys of Baragon and Godzilla. The later items, priced at nearly four times the price of the vinyl toys, sold only moderately well and were then shelved for several years.

The following year added Minya, Gorosaurus, MechaniKong, and King Kong (although titled Giant Gorilla on the packaging) to the basic line, plus a King Kong wire controlled model kit. A large sized Plamodel Godzilla kit was also introduced. This was to be the last Godzilla toy that Marusan would produce, in part be-

Mattel's Godzilla Gang, the first line of Godzilla toys in the US.

cause the company was starting to fall on hard times financially. This toy was also expensive to produce and, in the end, would be the most limited release in the Marusan line.

Due to their failing finances, in 1968 Marusan neglected to add any new figures to the Godzilla line, missing out on a chance to release a King Ghidrah figure in conjunction with the release of *Destroy all Monsters* to the theaters. In fact, due to the increase in popularity of Gamera and the *UltraSeven* TV show and characters, Marusan would not even get the chance to release the last two figures in the Godzilla line that they had been working on (Gabara and a new Minya) before declining sales forced the company to close in early 1970.

Enter Bullmark, the salvation of the Godzilla toy line.

Bullmark bought up the molds from the defunct company. Sensing untapped potential they went to work, adding several new figures to the line (as well as Ultraman and the other monster lines). This proved to be the best possible move that they could make, as monster super heroes were becoming the rage on TV and kids were anxious to purchase as many as they could. While the revenues for the new Godzilla films were on the decline in the early 1970s, the audiences were becoming more and more preadolescent. These young viewers were as anxious as ever to see their hero on the screen and buy as many of his products as they could. Toho even started repackaging their earlier films with cartoons and other children's features and releas-

ing them in special 'festivals' to attract the younger audience.

Around this time, Asahi Sonorama started to issue children's book and record sets with each new movie, as well as when the older movies were repackaged in the festivals. These books sold fantastically well to the children who delighted in hearing the sound effects and songs from the movies at home (remember there were no soundtracks or VCR's yet). They also published story books with artwork depicting the monster battles the children wished they could have seen: Varan vs. Manda ... or perhaps Mothra vs. Mogera is more to your liking?

Needless to say, not only did these books sell well, but they continue to be highly prized by collectors today.

In 1970, Bullmark re-re-leased several of Marusan's older figures (Baragon, Mothra, Gorosaurus, MechaniKong, and Ebirah) as well as adding three of Godzilla's most popular costars to their line of standard vinyl toys: Angilas, Rodan, and Ghidrah. Adding to the line was the best possible move that they could have made, as these figures became very popular. Bullmark quickly followed the success of these figures with a couple of other Toho monsters that had not been released before, Varan and Mogera. Bullmark then added a limited release of large scale versions of three of their best sellers: Godzilla, Ghidrah, and Baragon. This Godzilla is the toy that was to be prominently featured in the opening scenes of Toho's next installment in the Godzilla series — *Godzilla vs. the Smog Monster*. Needless to say, they added a Smog Monster (Hedorah) figure to the line also.

For the holiday season in 1971, Bullmark chose to try and capture some of the higher disposable income market by releasing Marusan's Tin Toy series again. They also added Jirass to the line, a monster from the *Ultra-Man* series who was made from an old Godzilla costume (the Godzilla mold could easily have been modified to make the new monster).

The year 1972 saw the release of *Godzilla vs. Gigan*. Of course a vinyl figure was soon to follow, as was another modification of the tin Godzilla mold to produce the newest monster. Because of some problems with the castings for the tin Gigan mold, it was only available for a very brief period in stores. It has become one of the hardest to find items in the Godzilla toy series.

Unfortunately, the great monster boom was on its last legs, as childrens' interest in monsters was waning, as it is prone to do. They were growing bored with their "old" toys and were moving on to newer and more exciting things. The next two Godzilla movies would see the worst attendance in the series forty plus year history. Bullmark still made vinyl toys of the new monsters from these films (Megalon and MechaGodzilla), but due to the fact that the standard size versions of these two figures were only available at theaters (thus becoming the first theater exclusive Godzilla toys), not many were produced and they have become the most sought after and the rarest of all Godzilla toys.

American collectors also finally saw their patience rewarded and two new Japanese monster items hit the toy shelves in the form of model kits from the Aurora company. Rodan and Ghidrah were the newest releases from Aurora's 'Monsters of the Movies' line. Sales of these kits (and the line as a whole), did not live up to Aurora's expectations and the entire line was canceled before a proposed and already prepared prototype new Godzilla kit could be released.

Lack of interest also forced Bullmark to quit producing vinyl monsters in 1975. They briefly tried to light the fire under their license for the Toho monsters one last time in 1977. Competitor Popy's line of die-cast robot figures called Shogun Warriors had become hugely popular in Japan, as had all things robot-related, and Bullmark decided to try and release their own versions of the Toho monsters in die-cast metal. Godzilla, Baragon, Ghidrah, MechaGodzilla, and Gigan were released as die-cast metal and rubber figures, all with firing missiles and assorted extra weapons. Sales on the line were not as strong as had been hoped for. Consequently, for their next release in the series, they produced an Angilas figure that was crafted more like a pure robot than a monster, closely resembling the competition's line. Unfortunately, this only served to drive the buyers away. The announced Mothra and Mogera die-cast figures were never to be produced, and this beautifully rendered series figure was to be the last that Bullmark would manufacture before going bankrupt.

In 1978, Popy bought up most of the licenses from the bankrupt Bullmark company. They too released their own line of Godzilla toys, but they tried to avoid some of Bullmark's mistakes by releasing more serious looking monsters. Chief among these was the "Jumbosaurus," the first really large Godzilla toy made and the first to make a realistic Godzilla roar. It remains to this day one of the most popular and sought after toys. Popy's toys appealed not only to children, but to the emerging adult collector's market. The first generation of children to see Godzilla at the movies had now grown up and, with increasing discretionary income, many had grown nostalgic and started searching for objects reminding them of their childhood.

Unfortunately, without any new movies to support them, or continuous showings on TV, the small base of collectors was not large enough to sustain a whole toy line. Popy discontinued making Godzilla toys to focus on their more profitable lines. Mattel tried to duplicate Popy's overseas success with the Shogun Warriors line here in America, and even bought the rights to some of their vinyl designs to try and capitalize on the newly released Godzilla cartoon shown on Saturday mornings,

but it was a half-hearted and failed effort. The 'Godzilla's Gang' figures, as they were called, certainly had a Godzilla figure in them, but since the cartoon had no other Toho monsters featured in it, Mattel declined to purchase rights to any of the other monsters. Instead Mattel used molds of characters from the "Ultra" series which was so popular in Japan at the time but was totally unknown to children in America. The Shogun Warrior line suffered a similar fate. The toys just were not as well made and did not have the play value here that they did in Japan. The line folded after just a few short years, but not without adding two more figures to the ranks of sought after Godzilla toys. They issued a Godzilla figure loosely based on the Jumbosaurus figure; however, the new figure lacked any back fins (replaced with a few crude lumps) or a roar, and included a "flame tongue." The last figure Mattel issued was a beautiful Rodan piece with a wingspan of over three feet. Wisely, they chose to leave the Shogun Warriors name off of the box, instead labeling Rodan under the banner of "The World's Greatest Monsters" Se-

Godzilla vs. King Ghidora, the start of the 1990s boom in all things Godzilla.

ries (even though it was the only "world's greatest monster" ever released).

Toys took a noticeable lapse from the spotlight for the next few years, with a few odds and ends from Beetland being the only truly active licensee releasing new products. The most notable items released during this period were books, of all things! With the release of Asahi Sonorama's *Fantastic Collection #5 — Godzilla*, as well as Kodansha's *Complete Collection of Godzilla*, fans finally had access to behind the scenes information and pictures that they had always dreamed of.

In 1982, the Japan SPFX Convention 2 was held in Tokyo. Garage kits were shown to the public for the first time and the eager buying adult collector was finally recognized. These early conventions in Japan were also the proving grounds for the collectible value of some of the earlier toys and merchandise produced. It was at these shows that Bullmark vinyl figures first started to be seen with the then outrageous price tags of $100 or more.

Finally, in 1983, with the release of the first new Godzilla movie in nearly a decade officially announced, Godzilla merchandising began what has been a quantum leap forward in not only items produced, but in the depth of variety also. It has been estimated that more different Godzilla items have been produced in the last decade than in the previous three combined! It was in 1983 that Yamakatsu released a line of seven highly collectible figures *and* that Bandai began what has become for collectors the greatest line of Godzilla figures yet produced. Bandai released more figures, in a greater variety of sizes, than any other manufacturer before them. They have certainly noticed the collectors market, going so far as to release limited repainted versions of their more popular figures in the past few years.

The year 1989 saw the release of *Godzilla vs. Biollante* from Toho. This was also the year for the reintroduction of a half-dozen classic Toho monsters from Bandai. Angilas, Megalon, Rodan, Gigan, MechaGodzilla, Ghidrah, and the Mothra larva were all released around this time with a re-release of a Godzilla figure that was supposed to look like his screen incarnation from 1964. They also chose to re-release the large size Godzilla they had released in 1984 as part of The Great Monsters Series (although in a slightly smaller scale), and would release a large Mothra larva the next year in much the same fashion.

Unsure of what the reaction would be to the totally new monster, Bandai chose not to make a Biollante at this time. The King Ghidrah figure from the Great Monster Series would never be re-released, probably due to the poorly designed wings which were almost guaranteed to break after being assembled for a time.

Starting in 1991, a new Godzilla movie was released every winter for the next five years, a rate of which had not been seen since the mid-1960s. Of course every winter, like clockwork, Bandai would release toys from the newest movie and, usually, a few of the classic monsters as well. With the release of the next film, *Godzilla vs. King Ghidora*, Bandai wisely chose to release the newly updated versions of both Godzilla and King Ghidora as seen in the film, plus a larger version of the new Mecha-King Ghidora and Godzilla to go with him.

The following year saw (along with the release of the remake of *Godzilla vs. Mothra*) Bandai issue vinyl figures for the original Mothra, a Biollante figure (finally),

Minya, Baragon, and MechaKong (from *King Kong Escapes*), as well as newly updated versions of Mothra (both larva and adult stages), and the new monster Battra. This was also the year that Bandai would release a repainted set of ten Bullmark figures, introducing a new generation of fans to the toys of their parents.

In 1993, the greatest numbers of Bandai vinyl figures to date were released, with not only the release of figures from the new film *Godzilla vs. MechaGodzilla*, but also figures of Godzillasaurus, Gorosaurus, Hedora, Kamakiras, King Caesar, King Kong, and Jet Jaguar. That year also saw the release of what is perhaps the crowning achievement in a Godzilla figure series, the release of the first Tokyo Marui radio controlled Godzilla figure. As of this writing, 1993 and the previous year would be the pinnacle of popularity for Godzilla toys in the nineties.

The next two years would see a slowdown in the release of vinyl figures and an upturn in the release of battery-operated and higher end figures like the Deluxe Series (Godzilla, Mogera, SpaceGodzilla and Destroyer), and the Real Action Series (1954, 1993, 1995 style Godzillas, SpaceGodzilla and Destroyer).

The creativity of Bandai seemed to have already peaked, as 1996 brought the issuance of re-painted figures in the Godzilla Forever Series and in the Godzilla Memorial box. In fact, for the first time in the 1990s, Bandai would release no new figures in the Godzilla line in 1996.

Fortunately, collectors would not have to go without. For at this time, America finally had a Godzilla line to call its own. Released by the Trendmasters Corporation, American Godzilla fans were able to purchase Godzilla and all his friends (and enemies) in great abundance at their local toy store. Available for the first time from an American manufacturer were toy figures of Varan, Mothra, Gigan, Angilas, Biollante and all the new monsters whose films had yet to be shown in the states. At the time this book was written, Trendmasters' plans called for an even greater expansion of the line to coincide with the May 1998 release of the first filmed-in-America Godzilla movie.

Not to be outdone by their American counterparts, several smaller Japanese companies have picked up the slack let out by Bandai. Marmit, a relatively new company to the toy business, and M-1—long noted as being a producer of great Godzilla vinyl kits (as well as being owned by a lifelong Godzilla fanatic)—have both announced plans to produce a line of Godzilla (and other companies') vinyl figures, including many figures that have not ever been produced as toys.

The future of Godzilla collectibles looks bright indeed.

Chapter 3

Market Overview

'On fire' is the best way to describe the current state of the Godzilla toy market. The collector's market expanded at a phenomenal rate in 1996, with scores of new collectors entering the field. This expansion almost coincided with the decision of toy manufacturer Bandai to STOP producing the majority of their toy line. As can be imagined, this created an incredible demand for both long out of production and newly out of production figures. Items that had in the previous year been available at close-out prices, such as Biollante, were suddenly found to be in tremendous demand. New collectors were scrambling to acquire pieces which had long been neglected. It now seems as if record prices are being reported almost weekly. The most noted example of this occurred in early 1996, when Bandai released a special limited edition 'Burning Godzilla' to movie theaters in Japan. This figure, originally priced at the U.S. equivalent of about $20, soon was being sold in the states for anywhere between $70 and $150.

Hopefully, as more dealers enter the market and contacts with Japanese sources become more concrete, these sorts of price fluctuations will decrease and prices will settle down to more acceptable levels. The market has, in fact, shown some signs of doing just that. A later, identical theater promotion by Bandai for the newest Gamera movie resulted in a toy that sold for a more respectable $40-$60.

The demand for the Bandai figures in the past two years, has been so great that prices were beginning to approach (and in some cases pass) the lofty heights usually reserved for the toys of yesteryear—the Popys and the Bullmarks. Many collectors who were then new to the field had never even seen a Bullmark or a Popy toy as many dealers very rarely stocked them. Dealers stayed away from these toys, unsure of their salability and unable to research their history as most all available information was in Japanese. Two years ago, the number of American dealers who stocked vintage Japanese monster toys could be counted on one hand, but now many major cities have at least one store with a nice selection.

Although there are still collectors who try to collect everything, most collectors narrow their attention on one specific area and will only occasionally venture into something else. The most widely available line today is the American Trendmasters line, available at almost every toy store in America.

For Japanese toys, the king of the hill is Bandai, the company that has produced the largest line of Godzilla toys to date. However, once collectors finish their standard Bandai collection and as they gather more information, most turn to the older toys and the roots of Godzilla collecting.

Many dealers, once shy about carrying the higher priced and scarcer older toys, have bowed to customer demand and started stocking them. It is only natural for collectors to want to learn more about, and then collect, the earlier toys. Most peoples' first vision of a Bullmark toy comes while watching *Godzilla vs. the Smog Monster*, as Ken Yano pushes a pair of Godzilla toys down his slide. Most Americans are stunned to learn what the Japanese have taken for granted, that these were not props made for the movies but actually toys that one could purchase.

With that in mind, let's look at some specific areas and manufacturers.

Marusan/Bullmark

Synonymous in the minds of many collectors with the rarest and most expensive toys, many are finding out that with the recent price increases in many of the newer toy lines, these companies' products represent a surprisingly affordable yet challenging line to collect. True, the rarest and most expensive items are from these two companies, but many collectors are searching for at least one or two representative examples to add to their collections. Crude by today's standards, these toys nonetheless represent the "Golden Age of Godzilla." They are the most historically important and most desirable of all the Godzilla toys.

Popy

Popy was the third company to create a line of Godzilla toys. It was also the first to try and offer more realistic versions of the monsters, instead of the characterizations that Marusan and Bullmark had offered. Popy is most noted for the release of the "Jumbosaurus," the first really large scale Godzilla toy and the first to feature a realistic Godzilla roar.

Bandai

Bandai produced the largest and most widely collected Godzilla toy line. The company first made a trio of Godzilla models in 1971. Then it did not enter the field again until 1983, when the firm started what has been the most successful of all the Godzilla toy lines. These figures form the core of most enthusiasts' collections.

Yamakatsu/Yutaka/Misc.

Yamakatsu toys have finally started to come into their own. This line originally came out at the same time as the first Bandai toys, but has long been ignored by collectors. With the rising prices on the Bandai figures, collectors are waking up to how undervalued these figures really are. Yutaka toys have always been in demand by collectors of the smaller type figures and look to continue to be popular in the future.

Posters/Paper Material

Arguably the most difficult of all areas to collect (with the exception of actual movie props), paper material is possibly the most fragile and difficult to store, and yet it is also the earliest and rarest of all Godzilla collectibles. Remember, the first images the public ever saw of our favorite monster were those posters hanging outside the movie theaters. Toho has been very frugal when it comes to releasing posters and stills. Only a precious few of the early ones have reached American shores.

Top Ten Lists

Taking into account the public's appetite for ranking (always wanting to know what is the most valuable, the rarest, etc.), we have compiled a list of what we think the ten rarest Godzilla toys and posters. Due to the fact that Bandai vinyl toys are in such demand and that none of them make the list, we have created a separate top ten list for them.

Ten Rarest Toys		Price
1	Marusan Plamodel Large Scale Godzilla	$8,000+
2	Marusan Plamodel Ebirah	7,000+
3	Marusan Plamodel Baragon	6,000+
4	Marusan Plamodel Godzilla	5,000+
5	Marusan Plamodel Hatching Minya	2,000+
6	Bullmark Remote Control Gigan	3,000
7	Marusan Vinyl Giant Gorilla	2,500
8	Bullmark Vinyl Megalon (standard size)	2,000
9	Bullmark Vinyl MechaGodzilla (standard size)	2,000
10	Bullmark Vinyl Hedora (pink color)	1,500

Ten Rarest Posters (One Sheets)		Price
1	Godzilla 1 sheet (B style)	$3,500
2	Gigantis 1 sheet (B style)	2,000
3	Gigantis 1 sheet (A style)	3,000
4	Godzilla 1 sheet (A style)	4,000
5	Godzilla 1957 Japanese 1 sheet	2,500
6	Godzilla 1957 International style 1 sheet	1,200
7	Gigantis 1955 International style 1 sheet	700
8	King Kong vs. Godzilla Jap. 1 sheet	1,100
9	Godzilla Polish 1 sheet	700
10	Godzilla Spanish 1 sheet	500

Ten Toughest Standard Bandai Vinyl Figures		Price
1	1962 Godzilla	$225
2	1964 King Ghidrah	175
3	1984 Godzilla	175
4	1992 Mothra Larva	150
5	1974 Mecha-Godzilla (original 1983 version)	125
6	1961 Mothra Adult	100
7	Biollante	250
8	1964 Godzilla (original 1983 version)	100
9	Baragon	175
10	1991 Godzilla ('closed mouth')	125

Godzilla—All the Collectibles

Chapter 4

Bob Eggleton-
Cover painting to
Godzilla #11 (Dark
Horse Comics).
$1,500-2,500.

ACTIVITY ITEMS

Balls

AI1001	Madballs Set (3" Bandai, 1993)(Godzilla, MechaGodzilla)ea.	$5-10
AI1101	Madballs Set (2" Bandai, 1996)(Godzilla, Little Godzilla, Burning Godzilla, Mothra, MechaGodzilla)	ea. 4-8
AI1201	Godzilla Top-Flite Golf Balls (Spalding, 1991)	10 -15
AI1301	Toho Set (3", Toho 1994)(Godzilla, King Ghidora, MechaGodzilla, Mothra)	ea. 4-8

Guns

AI2001	Godzilla Raids Again Spring Rifle (1950s)	$450-700
AI2101	Godzilla Target Set (Yamakatsu)	60-100
AI2201	Godzilla Water Gun (Yutaka)	10-15

Kites

AI3001	Godzilla	$10-15
AI3101	Godzilla (Yamakatsu, 1978)	25-40
AI3102	Destroy All Monsters (Yamakatsu, 1988)	20-30
AI3201	Godzilla vs. MechaGodzilla (Toho, 1993)	15-25

Above: Left to Right: AI1301 Toho ball set, each $4-8. AI1001, 1101 Madballs, each $4-10. AI1201 Godzilla Top-Flite Golf Balls, box $10-15.

Left: AI3101 Godzilla kite by Yamakatsu. $25-40.

ARTWORK, ORIGINAL

Animation cels and comic book artwork are nearly impossible to put an accurate average price on, as each piece is different and has a unique value. Some of the most important points to consider are: the age of the piece (art from the 1950s and '60s is much more difficult to acquire than art from the 1970s and '80s), the popularity of the artist (a painting by the award winning artist Bob Eggleton will sell for much more than a piece done by a more obscure fan), medium (all things being equal, a painting is worth more than an ink drawing, which is worth more than a pencil sketch), and what the art was done for (a painting for a movie poster will be worth more than a painting for a magazine, which will be worth more than pen and ink work for a comic book). One rule that is universal is that published work is always worth more than non-published. Just make sure that you are comparing apples with apples when attempting to value artwork. Even a non-published pencil sketch by Frank Frazetta will be worth more than a published painting by almost anyone else. Most importantly, remember, as with almost everything, the price is determined by what the buyer is willing to pay and what the seller will take. Since there is only one of any given piece in existence, its value will always vary from person to person. What might be one person's favorite image will be another's least liked. With that in mind, we will attempt to list some average prices that work by some of the more popular artists who have drawn Godzilla might sell for. We will also provide some guidelines to use when evaluating animation art.

Artist Name	Pages	Covers	Paintings
Adams, Art	$50-100	$200-400	
Eggleton, Bob	70-125	1000-2000	$1500-2500
McKinny, Brandon	20-50	100-200	
Scalf, Chris		100-200	
Trimpe, Herb	10-50	100-300	

Original artwork for the cover to *Godzilla #3* (Dark Horse Comics) by Art Adams. $200-400.

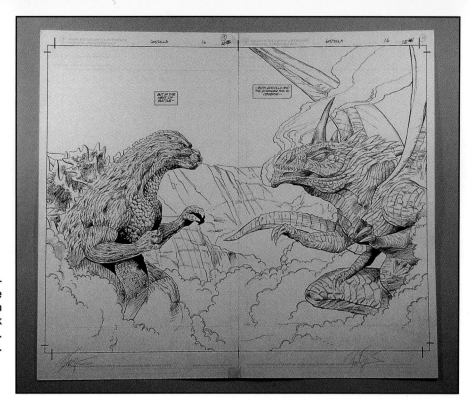

Bob Eggleton-
Double page
spread from
Godzilla #16 (Dark
Horse Comics).
$150-200.

ANIMATION CELS

As with other artwork, each animation cel is unique. The ranges given depend on the size of the image on the cel, the quality of the scene, and the level of preservation. Backgrounds tend to be rarer and more expensive than cels because several cels would be used over one background scene. Cels from the opening credits or title sequence tend to be the most valuable and hardest to find as only one sequence was used for an entire season.

AN1001	Backgrounds	$200-400
AN1002	Godzilla	75-150
AN1003	Godzooky	50-100
AN1004	Misc. (ship crew & other characters)	30-60
AN1005	Titles	300 +

AN1002 Godzilla animation cel from the 1978 cartoon. $75-150.

AN1003 Godzooky Animation cel (w/background). $250-500 (cel and background).

AN1005 Title cel from *The Godzilla Power Hour*. $300+

AUTOGRAPHS

This is another difficult subject to deal with. Autographs are very popular with collectors, but unless you live in or can travel to Japan, they can be very difficult to obtain. We have listed prices only for some of the more sought after autographs from people associated with the films who are deceased.

Ichiro Arishima	$20-40
Ishiro Honda	50-100
Tetsuko Koyayashi	20-40
Takashi Shimura	40-80
Tomoyuki Tanaka	40-80
Jun Tazaki	20-40
Eiji Tsuburaya	100-200

BADGES/PINS/BUTTONS

Badges/patches

BA1001	Godzilland (4 different, 1993)	$10-15
BA1002	Godzilla (breathing fire, 1993)	10-15
BA1003	Godzilla (caricature, 1993)	10-15
BA1004	Mothra (larva, 1993)	10-15
BA1005	Godzilla vs. King Ghidora (set of 3)	25-35
BA1006	Godzilla vs. MechaGodzilla Passkit	6-12
BA1007	Godzilla vs. Mothra (set of 3)	35-45
BA1008	G-Force Passkit (1995)	5-10

Pins

Cinema Shares (pin-backs)

BA2001	Godzilla, Megalon, Jet Jaguar, Gigan (theater give-away)	ea. $15-20

Concorde (Lit-Godzi, enamel)

BA3001	Baby Godzilla	$6-10
BA3002	Godzilla	6-10

Pil (pin-backs)

BA4001	Godzilla, King of the Monsters (2" dia.)	$3-5
BA4002	SD Godzilla (1 1/2" dia.)	3-5
BA4003	SD MechaGodzilla (1 1/2" dia.)	3-5
BA4004	SD Minya (1 1/2" dia.)	3-5

New Creations (enamel)

BA5001	Godzilla	$5-9
BA5002	Godzilla (silhouette w/40th anniversary)	5-9
BA5003	Godzilla (40th Anniversary logo only)	5-9
BA5004	Godzilla vs. MechaGodzilla	5-9
BA5005	MechaGodzilla 1993	5-9
BA5006	MechaGodzilla (head only)	5-9
BA5007	MechaGodzilla (Godzilla silhouette)	5-9
BA5008	Rodan 1993	5-9
BA5009	SuperGodzilla	5-9

Takara (pin-backs, 1991 1 1/2" dia.)

BA6001	King Ghidora, Godzilla, poster style, SD Godzilla	ea. $6-10

Yamakatsu (Godzilland Series pin-backs, 1984, 1" dia.)

BA7001	Godzilla, Minya, King Ghidora, MechaGodzilla, Mogera, Rodan, Mothra, Hedorah, Angilas, and Godzilland logo	ea. $5-10

BANKS

BN1001	Godzilla (Beetland, 1983)	$150-200
BN1101	Godzilla (tin-plate, U.S., 80s)	25-40
BN1201	Godzilla, SD (12" tall, Yutaka)	60-90
BN1202	Godzilla, Burning SD (12" tall, Yutaka)	60-90
BN1203	Godzilla, SD (5" tall, Yutaka)	15-25
BN1204	Godzilla, Burning SD (5" tall, Yutaka)	15-25
BN1301	Godzilla (monster sound series)	50-75
BN1302	King Ghidora (monster sound series)	50-75
BN1401	Godzilla Bust Spinning Bank (Everlast, 1993)	20-30
BN1501	LitGodzi Series (1995)	
	Godzilla, Destroyer, King Ghidora, MechaGodzilla, Mothra (larva & adult), Rodan, SpaceGodzilla	ea. 12-17
BN1601	Sound Series (7" tall, Banpresto, 1996)	
	Godzilla, Mothra (larva), King Ghidora	ea. 25-40

BA5001-5009 New Creations Enamel pins. Each $5-9.

BN1001 Godzilla bank. $150-200.

BN1301 and 1302 Godzilla and King Ghidora monster sound banks. Each $50-75.

BN1401 LitGodzi series banks. Left to Right: King Ghidora, Baby Godzilla, Godzilla and MechaGodzilla. Each $12-17.

BOOKS/MAGAZINES

BOOKS –
Japanese Books

Abura Shobo
BO0001　Godzilla and Giant Monsters Talking Picture Book
(1993, ¥2800)　　$30-50

Asahi Sonorama
BO0101　All About the World of Monsters-Fantastic Collection
Special　(1981, ¥2300)　　$30-50
BO0102　Birth of Godzilla (1994, ¥1800)　　15-30
BO0103　Cinema Monstology (1993, ¥1400)　　12-20
BO0104　Destroy All Monsters-Sono Sheet (1970, ¥380)　　70-120
BO0105　Eiji Tsuburaya-The Director of Special Effects　(1993, ¥9500)90-140
BO0106　Giant Monster Shock-Sono Sheet (1970, ¥490)　　80-130
BO0107　Godzilla Battles Super Picture Book-Uchusen Ultra Books
(1992, ¥1000)　　10-20
BO0108　Godzilla-Fantastic Collection #5 (1978, ¥500)　　20-30
BO0109　Godzilla Graffiti-Fantastic Collection #30 (1983, ¥550)　　15-25
BO0110　Godzilla-Sono Sheet #1 (1979, ¥350)　　20-30
BO0111　Godzilla-Sono Sheet #2 (1979, ¥350)　　20-30
BO0112　Godzilla vs. Space Godzilla Postcard Book (1994, ¥520)　　5-12
BO0113　Godzilla vs. Hedorah-Sono Sheet (1971, ¥490)　　60-90
BO0114　Godzilla vs. Space Godzilla Super Picture Book -Uchusen
Ultra Books　(1994, ¥1000)　　10-20
BO0201　Godzilla (84) Uchusen Pocket Book (1984, ¥520)　　10-20
BO0202　Godzilla vs. Biollante Uchusen Pocket Book (1989, ¥650)　　10-20
BO8001　Godzilla vs. King Ghidora Uchusen Pocket Book (1991, ¥720)10-20
BO8002　Godzilla vs. Mothra Uchusen Pocket Book (1992, ¥850)　　10-20
BO8003　Godzilla vs. MechaGodzilla Uchusen Pocket Book (1993, ¥850)10-20
BO8004　Godzilla vs. Space Godzilla Uchusen Pocket Book (1994, ¥850)10-20
BO8005　Godzilla vs. Destroyer-Uchusen Extra (1995, ¥1200)　　10-20
BO0115　Heisei Version-Giant Monster Newest Super Picture Book-
Uchusen Ultra Books (1992, ¥800)　　10-20
BO0116　King of the Monsters Godzilla (1995, ¥1700)　　15-30
BO0117　Monster Anatomy (1967)　　75-125
BO0118　Monsters Super Powers Super Picture Book -Uchusen Ultra
Books (1993, ¥1000)　　12-25
BO0119　SFX Godzilla-Fantastic Collection #44 (1984, ¥650)　　8-15
BO0120　Toho SFX Monster Movie Encyclopedia (1989, ¥12000)　100-200
BO0121　Toho SFX Movie Poster Collection #1 (postcard book)
(1984, ¥580)　　6-12
BO0122　Toho SFX Movie Poster Collection #2 (postcard book)
(1984, ¥580)　　6-12
BO0123　3D Monster Catalog-Fantastic Collection #38 (1984, ¥550)　6-12
BO0124　Wonderful SFX Movie World　(1979, ¥500)　　15-25
BO0125　World of Special Effects in Japan　(1980, ¥2500)　　50-75

Aspect
BO0201　Godzilla Museum　(1994, ¥2000)　　$25-35

Bandai
BO8101　Bandai Entertainment Bible #7-New Godzilla Encyclopedia
(1990, ¥850)　　$8-15
BO8102　Bandai Entertainment Bible #41-New Godzilla Encyclopedia
(1991, ¥880)　　8-15
BO8103　Bandai Entertainment Bible #50-New Godzilla Encyclopedia
(1992, ¥880)　　8-15
BO0301　Godzilla-Cult Quest 500 (1992, ¥680)　　15-25
BO0302　Godzilla Toy Museum (1992, ¥5000)　　70-100
BO0303　Gunhead Catalog (1989, ¥1000)　　10-20
BO0304　SFX Gunhead Photo Book　(1988, ¥700)　　7-15

Chikuma Shobo
BO0401　Good Morning Godzilla (1992, ¥2200)　　$20-30
BO0402　Inside Godzilla (Ken Satsuma story) (1993, ¥1100)　　10-20
BO0403　Shining Fairies and Mothra (1994, ¥1600)　　15-25

Chukei Shuppan
BO0501　Study of the Godzilla Era (1992, ¥1300)　　$20-30

Cinema Jumpo
BO0601　Monster Collection (1967)　　$100-200

Dai Nippon Kaiga
BO3004　Godzilla First (1994, ¥3600)　　$50-80
BO3003　Godzilla Second (1994, ¥3600)　　50-80
BO3001　Toho SFX Super Weapons Catalog　(1993, ¥2800)　　30-50

Data House
BO3051　Godzilla Collection, Toho Special　Effects Movie Poster
Collection　(1995, ¥2800)　　$30-50

Forest
BO0801　Making of Mothra (1996, ¥1800)　　$15-25

Futami Shobo
BO0901　99 Facts About Giant Monster Godzilla (1993, ¥480)　　$6-12
BO0902　Toho Monster Movie Series #1-Monster Zero (photo novel)
(1979, ¥390)　　12-25
BO0903　Toho Monster Movie Series　#2-Godzilla vs. MechaGodzilla
(photo novel)(1979, ¥390)　　12-25

Left to Right: BO0104 Destroy All Monsters
($70-120), BO0106 Giant Monster Shock ($80-
130), and BO0113 Godzilla vs. Hedorah ($60-90).

BO0302
Godzilla Toy
Museum.
$70-100.

BO8302-8303
Encyclopedia
of Godzilla
(King Ghidora
and Mothra
versions).
Each $22-35.

Left to Right: BO8401, 8403 *Giant Monster Godzilla* #'s 1 and 3. Each $20-30.

BO3101-3102 *Pictorial Book of Godzilla* Vol. One and Two. Each $50-70.

BO1203 *Revenge of Godzilla* comic. $10-20.
BO1201 *Declaration of Godzilla*. $15-25.

BO8602,8603 *Godzilla Magazine* #2 & 3. Each $6-10. BO8601 *Godzilla Magazine* #1. $10-20.
BO8607 *Godzilla Magazine* #7. $8-11.

Gakken

BO8301	*Encyclopedia of Godzilla* (Biollante version) (1989, ¥2000)	$22-35
BO8302	*Encyclopedia of Godzilla* (King Ghidora version) (1991, ¥2200)	22-35
BO8303	*Encyclopedia of Godzilla* (Mothra version) (1992, ¥2200)	22-35
BO8304	*Encyclopedia of Godzilla* (MechaGodzilla version) (1993, ¥2200)	22-35
BO8305	*Encyclopedia of Godzilla* (Space Godzilla version) (1994, ¥2200)	22-35
BO1001	*Everything About Godzilla Movies* (1993, ¥2000)	20-30
BO1002	*Godzilla All Monsters* (1993, ¥750)	10-20
BO1003	*We Love Godzilla Everytime* (1996, ¥1700)	20-30

Hikarinokuni

BO8401	*Giant Monster Godzilla* #1-Hikarinokuni TV Picture Book #233 (¥300)	$20-30
BO8402	*Giant Monster Godzilla* #2-Hikarinokuni TV Picture Book #239 (¥300)	20-30
BO8403	*Giant Monster Godzilla* #3-Hikarinokuni TV Picture Book #240 (¥300)	20-30

Hobby Japan

BO3101	*Hobby Japan Special Issue, Godzilla* (1993, ¥1800)	$15-30
BO3102	*Pictorial Book of Godzilla* (1995, ¥3800)	50-70
BO3103	*Pictorial Book of Godzilla #2* (1995, ¥3800)	50-70

Hoga Shoten

BO1101	*Monster March* (1967)	$100-200

JICC

BO1201	*Declaration of Godzilla* (1984, ¥1000)	$15-25
BO1202	*Godzilla Comic, The* (1991, ¥980)	10-20
BO1203	*Revenge of the Godzilla Comic* (1992, ¥980)	10-20

Jitsugyo no Nihonsha

BO1301	*Godzilla and My Movie Life-Ishiro Honda* (1993, ¥1800)	$20-30
BO1302	*Godzilla Color Album* (book & color photos)(1984, ¥880)	20-30
BO1303	*Godzilla Color Book* (1984, ¥750)	30-50

BO1304	*Godzilla vs. Biollante Encyclopedia-Young Selection Color Book* (1989, ¥780)	8-15
BO1305	*Godzilla vs. Mothra Encyclopedia-Young Selection Color Book* (1993, ¥780)	8-15
BO1306	*Godzilla vs. MechaGodzilla Encyclopedia-Young Selection Color Book* (1993, ¥880)	8-15
BO1307	*Godzilla vs. Space Godzilla Encyclopedia-Young Selection Color Book* (1994, ¥880)	8-15
BO1308	*Godzilla vs. Destroyer Encyclopedia-Young Selection Color Book* (1996, ¥880)	8-15
BO1309	*Movie World of Eiji Tsuburaya* (1983, ¥2800)	60-100

Kadokawa Shoten

BO1401	*Extreme Godzilla-ism* (1990)	$8-15
BO1402	*Godzilla 1990* (comic) (1990, ¥800)	8-15
BO1403	*Way of Godzilla* (1995, ¥1400)	12-20

Keibunsha

BO1501	*Godzilla Battle Encyclopedia #555* (1993, ¥720)	$8-15
BO1502	*Godzilla Encyclopedias* (1972, ¥500)	100-200
BO1503	*Godzilla Encyclopedia #208* (1984, ¥650)	20-30
BO8601	*Godzilla Magazine* Vol.1 (1992, ¥680)	10-20
BO8602	*Godzilla Magazine* Vol.2 (1993, ¥680)	6-10
BO8603	*Godzilla Magazine* Vol.3 (1993, ¥700)	6-10
BO8604	*Godzilla Magazine* Vol.4 (1994, ¥740)	7-10
BO8605	*Godzilla Magazine* Vol.5 (1994, ¥740)	7-10
BO8606	*Godzilla Magazine* Vol.6 (1994, ¥740)	7-10
BO8607	*Godzilla Magazine* Vol.7 (1996, ¥760)	8-11
BO1504	*Godzilla Monster Battles Guide Book* (Super Famicom) (1993, ¥750)	5-10
BO8701	*Godzilla vs. King Ghidora Encyclopedia #477* (1992, ¥720)	10-15
BO8702	*Godzilla vs. Mothra Encyclopedia #517* (1993, ¥720)	10-15
BO8703	*Godzilla vs. MechaGodzilla Encyclopedia #564* (1994, ¥720)	9-14
BO8704	*Godzilla vs. SpaceGodzilla Encyclopedia #586* (1995, ¥730)	8-13
BO8705	*Godzilla vs. Destroyer Encyclopedia #602* (1996, ¥730)	8-13
BO1505	*Godzilla World of Giant Monsters-Color Series #8* (1984, ¥480)	15-20
BO1506	*Godzilla World* (comic) (1993, ¥680)	8-14
BO1507	*Mothra Encyclopedia #615* (1996, ¥760)	8-14
BO1508	*Super Godzilla Guide Book* (Super Famicom) (1993, ¥750)	5-10

Kindaibungeisha

BO1601	*Godzilla At Last Dies a Peaceful Death* (1995, ¥1200)	$12-20

Kindai Eigasha

BO8801	*Special Graffix-Godzilla vs. Biollante* (1989, ¥1500)	$20-30
BO8802	*Special Graffix-Godzilla vs. King Ghidora* (1991, ¥1500)	20-30
BO8803	*Special Graffix-Godzilla vs. Mothra* (1992, ¥1600)	20-30
BO8804	*Special Graffix-Godzilla vs. MechaGodzilla* (1993, ¥1700)	20-30
BO8805	*Special Graffix-Godzilla vs. SpaceGodzilla* (1994, ¥1800)	20-30
BO8806	*Special Graffix-Godzilla vs. Destroyer* (1995, ¥1800)	20-30
BO8807	*Special Graffix-Mothra* (1996, ¥1800)	20-30
BO1701	*Star Boy #1-Japanese SF Film Encyclopedia* (1979, ¥550)	12-20
BO1702	*Toho Monster Graffiti* (1991, ¥1500)	15-25
BO1703	*Toho SFX Movie Encyclopedia* (1994, ¥1980)	22-35

Kita Shoten

BO1801	*Godzilla vs. The Thing* Movie Comic (1985, ¥790)	$8-15
BO1802	*Godzilla vs. The Sea Monster* Movie Comic (85, ¥790)	8-15
BO1803	*Ghidrah, The Three-Headed Monster* Movie Comic (1985, ¥790)	8-15
BO1804	*Terror of MechaGodzilla* Movie Comic (1985, ¥790)	8-15
BO1805	*Godzilla (84)* Movie Comic (1985, ¥790)	8-15
BO1806	*Japanese SFX Monster Encyclopedia* (1985, ¥650)	10-18

Kodansha

BO1901	*All About Godzilla -TV Magazine Special* (1994, ¥3800)	$45-60
BO1902	*Complete Collection of Godzilla* (1979, ¥560)	20-30
BO1903	*Giant Monster Godzilla-Enjoyable Picture Book #27* (1979, ¥250)	20-35
BO1904	*Giant Monster Godzilla-Let's Play* (1979, ¥250)	15-30
BO1905	*Godzilla Giant Monsters-Kodansha Pocket Cards #1* (1979, ¥680)	40-80
BO1906	*Godzilla's Dinosaur Encyclopedia* (1979, ¥280)	20-40
BO1907	*Godzilla vs. Mothra* (comic) (1993, ¥400)	6-10
BO1908	*Godzilla vs. MechaGodzilla* (comic) (1993, ¥370)	6-10
BO1909	*Godzilla vs. Mothra-Comic BonBon Special #85* (1992, ¥1580)	15-25
BO1910	*Godzilla vs. MechaGodzilla Comic BonBon Special #89* (1993, ¥1680)	15-25
BO1911	*Godzilla-Super Mook #1* (1979, ¥480)	20-30
BO9901	*Godzilla vs. King Ghidora-Hit Books #20* (1991, ¥1600)	20-30
BO9902	*Godzilla vs. Mothra-Hit Books #30* (1992, ¥1600)	20-30
BO9903	*Godzilla vs. MechaGodzilla-Hit Books #43* (1993, ¥1800)	20-30
BO9904	*Godzilla vs. SpaceGodzilla-Hit Books #46* (1994, ¥2000)	20-30
BO1912	*Godzilla Giant Monster Picture Encyclopedia-Manga Encyclopedia #31* (1995, ¥880)	8-15
BO1913	*Mothra Giant Monster Encyclopedia-Manga Encyclopedia #40* (1996, ¥880)	8-15
BO1914	*Godzilla Giant Monster Encyclopedia-Kodansha Pocket Encyclopedia Series #2* (1979, ¥500)	20-40
BO1915	*Knowledge Quiz Encyclopedia #2-Kodansha Pocket Encyclopedia Series #7* (1979, ¥500)	20-40
BO1916	*Godzilla All Monster Encyclopedia-Kodansha Pocket Encyclopedia Series #66* (1990, ¥500)	6-14
BO1917	*Godzilla Monster Encyclopedia-Kodansha Pocket Encyclopedia Series #72* (1991, ¥550)	6-12
BO1918	*Godzilla vs. MechaGodzilla Seal Book #16* (1993, ¥700)	6-12
BO1919	*Godzilla King of the Monsters Picture Book-TV Magazine Color Book #9* (1979, ¥280)	20-35
BO1920	*Godzilla Giant Monsters-TV Magazine Color Book #12* (1979, ¥280)	20-35
BO8901	*Godzilla Graph Book-TV Magazine Deluxe #22* (1983, ¥850)	8-15
BO8902	*Godzilla Giant Monster Super Encyclopedia-TV Magazine Deluxe #20* (1992, ¥880)	10-20
BO8903	*Godzilla Giant Monster Super Encyclopedia-TV Magazine Deluxe #24* (1992, ¥880)	10-20
BO8904	*Godzilla Giant Monster Super Encyclopedia-TV Magazine Deluxe #28* (1992, ¥880)	10-20
BO8905	*Godzilla Giant Monster Super Encyclopedia-TV Magazine Deluxe #43* (1993, ¥950)	10-20
BO8906	*Godzilla Giant Monster Super Encyclopedia-TV Magazine Deluxe #54* (1994, ¥950)	10-20
BO8907	*Godzilla Giant Monster Super Encyclopedia-TV Magazine Deluxe #59* (1995, ¥1000)	10-20
BO8908	*Godzilla Giant Monster Super Encyclopedia-TV Magazine Deluxe #63* (1995, ¥1000)	10-20
BO8909	*Mothra Giant Monster Super Encyclopedia-TV Magazine Deluxe #70* (1996, ¥1000)	10-20
BO9001	*King of the Monsters Godzilla-TV Magazine Great #5* (1993, ¥580)	6-12
BO9002	*Godzilla vs. MechaGodzilla-TV Magazine Great #19* (1993, ¥580)	6-12
BO9003	*Godzilla All Monsters-TV Magazine Great #31* (1994, ¥620)	6-12
BO9004	*Godzilla vs. SpaceGodzilla-TV Magazine Great #42* (1995, ¥620)	6-12
BO9005	*Godzilla Picture Book (panorama)-TV Magazine Great #44* (1995, ¥620)	6-12
BO9006	*Godzilla vs. Destroyer-TV Magazine Great #65* (1996, ¥620)	6-12
BO9007	*Mothra-TV Magazine Great #83* (1996, ¥620)	6-12
BO1921	*King of the Monsters Godzilla-TV Magazine Poster Book #8* (1996, ¥550)	6-11
BO1922	*Godzilla-Film Album #1* (1979, ¥980)	8-16
BO1923	*Godzilla-TV Picture Book #7* (1984, ¥330)	20-30
BO9101	*Godzilla Giant Monsters-TV Picture Book #395* (1990, ¥340)	5-10
BO9102	*Godzilla vs. Mothra-TV Picture Book #595* (1992, ¥380)	4-8
BO9103	*Godzilla Big Battles-TV Picture Book #602* (1993, ¥380)	4-8
BO9104	*Godzilla vs. MechaGodzilla-TV Picture Book #690* (1993, ¥400)	4-8
BO9105	*Godzilla vs. Giant Monsters-TV Picture Book #694* (1994, ¥400)	4-8
BO9106	*Godzilla vs. SpaceGodzilla-TV Picture Book #764* (1994, ¥400)	4-8
BO9107	*Godzilla Giant Monster Deadly Battle Techniques-TV Picture Book #771* (1995, ¥400)	4-8
BO9108	*Godzilla vs. Destroyer-TV Picture Book #851* (1995, ¥400)	4-8
BO9109	*Godzilla Super Battle Collection-TV Picture Book #854* (1995, ¥400)	4-8
BO9110	*Mothra-TV Picture Book #944* (1996, ¥400)	4-8

BO8802-8805 *Special Graffix* series (pictured: SpaceGodzilla, King Ghidora, Mothra and MechaGodzilla). Each $20-30.

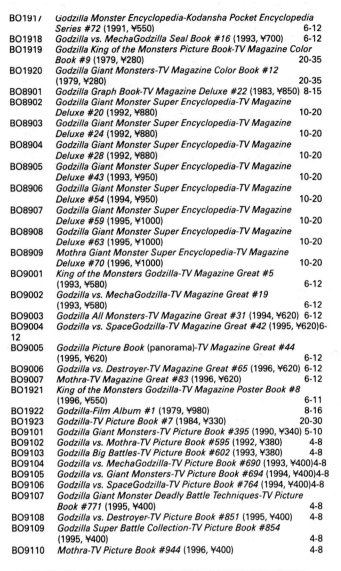

BO9003 and 9006 *Godzilla TV Magazine Great* #31 and #65. Each $6-12.

Above:
BO9108-9109.
Godzilla TV Picture Book #'s 851 and 854. Each $4-8.

Right: BO2903 *Films of Eiji Tsuburaya.* $300-500

BO2102, BO2101 *Enjoyable Monsters* and *All Monster Pictorial.* Each $80-120.

Clockwise from top left: BO8501, BO8505, BO8509, BO2905, BO2906 *Godzilla Books* #'s 1, 5 and 9. *Godzilla Books Extra* #'s 1 and 2. Each $10-20.

BO1924	*King of the Monsters Godzilla #1* (comic) (1992, ¥390)	4-8
BO1925	*King of the Monsters Godzilla #2* (comic) (1993, ¥390)	4-8
BO1926	*King of the Monsters Godzilla-SFX* (1993, ¥1500)	15-25
BO1927	*King of the Monsters Godzilla Diorama Picture Book-Comic BonBon Special #86* (1993, ¥680)	7-14
BO1928	*King of the Monsters Godzilla-TV Magazine Card Book #2* (1995, ¥980)	10-20
BO1929	*Look For Godzilla #1* (1993, ¥680)	7-12
BO1930	*Look For Godzilla #2* (1994, ¥680)	7-12
BO1931	*Look For Godzilla #3* (1994, ¥680)	7-12
BO1932	*New Godzilla Color Wide Graph* (1984, ¥600)	6-13

Kubo Shoten
BO2001	*Godzilla Monster Quiz Book* (1992, ¥680)	$7-14

Kurosaki Shuppan
BO2101	*All Monster Pictorial* (1972, ¥490)	$80-120
BO2102	*Enjoyable Monsters* (1971, ¥490)	80-120

Manga Oh
BO2201	*Monster Game Book* (1969)	$90-140

Media Works
BO2301	*Godzilla vs. G-Force* (1995, ¥1880)	$20-35

Movie YK
BO2401	*Godzilla vs. Biollante Postcard Collection* (1989, ¥600)	$7-14

Nagaoka Shoten
BO2501	*Godzilla* (1995, ¥400)	$5-10
BO2502	*Godzilla Big Battles* (1996, ¥400)	5-10
BO2503	*Mothra* (1996, ¥400)	4-8

Nesco
BO2601	*Godzilla Biology Introductory Theory* (1992, ¥1400)	$12-20

Nevus
BO2701	*Godzilla Pop-up Book* (1993, ¥1580)	$16-30
BO2702	*Legend of Godzilla Pop-up Book* (1994, ¥1580)	18-35

NTT Media Books
BO2801	*Godzilla Roars* (1993, ¥1200)	$10-20

Shogakukan
BO2901	*Films of Eiji Tsuburaya* (1973, ¥2200)	$300-500
BO2902	*Godzilla All Monster Encyclopedia-Korotan Book #104-85 & several reissues* (¥490)	5-10
BO2903	*Godzilla Introduction Encyclopedia Series #142-84 & several reissues* (¥520)	5-10
BO2904	*Godzilla Introduction Encyclopedia Series #150-84 & several reissues* (¥520)	5-10
BO8201	*Godzilla* (84-comic) (1984, ¥680)	10-20
BO8202	*Godzilla vs. Biollante* (comic) (1990, ¥370)	8-15
BO8203	*Godzilla vs. King Ghidora* (comic) (1991, ¥880)	8-15
BO8204	*Godzilla vs. Mothra* (comic) (1992, ¥880)	8-15
BO8205	*Godzilla vs. MechaGodzilla* (comic) (1993, ¥880)	8-15
BO8206	*Godzilla vs. SpaceGodzilla* (comic) (1994, ¥880)	8-15
BO8207	*Godzilla vs. Destroyer* (comic) (1995, ¥880)	8-15
BO8501	*Godzilla Appears!-Godzilla Books #1* (1983, ¥320)	10-20
BO8502	*Godzilla's Rampage-Godzilla Books #2* (1983, ¥320)	10-20
BO8503	*Godzilla vs. King Ghidrah-Godzilla Books #3* (1983, ¥320)	10-20
BO8504	*Godzilla vs. The Space Monsters-Godzilla Books #4* (1984, ¥320)	10-20
BO8505	*Godzilla vs. MechaGodzilla-Godzilla Books #5* (1984, ¥320)	10-20
BO8506	*Godzilla vs. The Earth Monsters-Godzilla Books #6* (1984, ¥320)	10-20
BO8507	*Godzilla vs. Mothra-Godzilla Books #7* (1984, ¥320)	10-20
BO8508	*Godzilla vs. Gigan-Godzilla Books #8* (1984, ¥320)	10-20
BO8509	*Godzilla Battle History-Godzilla Books #9* (1984, ¥320)	10-20
BO2905	*New Godzilla-Godzilla Books Extra #1* (1984, ¥320)	10-20
BO2906	*Godzilla Secrets-Godzilla Books Extra #2* (1984, ¥320)	10-20
BO2907	*Godzilla vs. Mothra Seal Book #1* (1992, ¥650)	7-14
BO2908	*Godzilla vs. MechaGodzilla Seal Book #2* (1993, ¥700)	7-14
BO2909	*Godzilla vs. SpaceGodzilla Seal Book #6* (1994, ¥700)	7-14
BO9201	*Godzilla vs. King Ghidora-TV Kun Deluxe* (1991, ¥1000)	10-20
BO9202	*Godzilla vs. Mothra-TV Kun Deluxe* (1992, ¥1000)	10-20
BO9203	*Godzilla vs. MechaGodzilla-TV Kun Deluxe* (1993, ¥1100)	10-20
BO9204	*Godzilla vs. SpaceGodzilla-TV Kun Deluxe* (1994, ¥1100)	10-20
BO9205	*Godzilla vs. Destroyer-TV Kun Deluxe* (1995, ¥1100)	10-20
BO9301	*Godzilla vs. King Ghidora-TV Picture Book* (1991, ¥380)	6-12
BO9302	*Godzilla vs. Mothra-TV Picture Book* (1992, ¥380)	6-12
BO9303	*Godzilla vs. MechaGodzilla-TV Picture Book* (1993, ¥400)	6-12
BO9304	*Godzilla vs. SpaceGodzilla-TV Picture Book* (1994, ¥400)	6-12
BO9305	*Godzilla vs. Destroyer-TV Picture Book* (1995, ¥400)	6-12
BO2910	*Making of Godzilla 1985* (1984, ¥1900)	30-50
BO2911	*Monster Planet Godzilla-TV Picture Book* (1994, ¥400)	8-12
BO2912	*Super Diorama Theater Godzilla* (1992, ¥1400)	15-25
BO2912	*3D Book-Monster Planet Godzilla-Shogakukan Color Wide Special* (1994, ¥880)	10-20

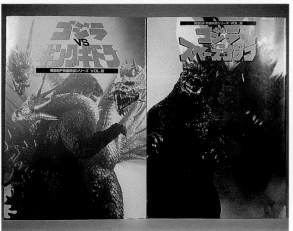

BO9506 *Toho SPFX Series #6 Godzilla vs. King Ghidora.* $20-35. BO9509 *Toho SPFX Series #9 Godzilla vs. Space Godzilla.* $25-40.

Shueisha
BO3001   *Godzilla Days* (1993, ¥2000) $20-35

Tachikaze Shobo
BO9402	*Godzilla Monster Encyclopedia* (1991, ¥470)	$6-12
BO9401	*Godzilla vs. Biollante Encyclopedia* (1989, ¥450)	6-12
BO9403	*Godzilla vs. King Ghidora Encyclopedia* (1991, ¥450)	6-12
BO9404	*Godzilla vs. Mothra Encyclopedia* (1992, ¥470)	6-12
BO9405	*Godzilla vs. MechaGodzilla Encyclopedia* (1993, ¥470)	6-12
BO9406	*Godzilla vs. SpaceGodzilla Encyclopedia* (1994, ¥470)	6-12
BO9407	*Godzilla vs. Destroyer Encyclopedia* (1995, ¥490)	6-12

Take Shobo
BO3101	*Godzilla Chronicles* (1993, ¥1800)	$20-35
BO3102	*Godzilla vs. King Ghidora Battle History Bamboo Comics* (1991, ¥880)	8-16
BO3103	*Godzilla vs. Mothra Battle History Bamboo Comics* (1992, ¥880)	8-16
BO3104	*Godzilla vs. MechaGodzilla Battle History Bamboo Comics* (1993, ¥880)	8-16

Takuma Orion
BO3201   *How Would You Like to Make Godzilla?-Koichi Kawakita SFX World* (1994, ¥1800) $18-30

Toho Publishing
BO3301	*Godzilla 40th Anniversary Postcards* (1993, ¥800)	$10-20
BO3302	*Godzilla vs. Destroyer Film Comic* (1995, ¥1300)	13-22
BO3303	*Toho SFX Movie Encyclopedia* (1983, ¥8500)	125-225
BO9501	*Toho Special Effects Series #1-Godzilla (84)* (1985, ¥1400)	15-25
BO9502	*Toho Special Effects Series #2-Godzilla vs. The Thing* (1985, ¥1800)	18-30
BO9503	*Toho Special Effects Series #3-Godzilla, Gigantis, Varan* (1985, ¥2000)	20-35
BO9504	*Toho Special Effects Series #4-Atragon, Gorath, Dogora The Space Monster* (1985, ¥2500)	25-40
BO9505	*Toho Special Effects Series #5-King Kong vs. Godzilla, Mysterians* (1986, ¥2500)	25-40
BO9506	*Toho Special Effects Series #6-Godzilla vs. King Ghidora*	

Right: BO3303 *Toho SFX Movie Encyclopedia.* $125-225.

Far right: Left to Right: BO3701, BO3704, and BO3702. *Godzilla Legend, Making of Godzilla Legend,* and *Godzilla Gaiden.* Each $7-20.

BO3601 and 3602. *Art of Godzilla* and *Art of Godzilla vs. Mothra.* Each $30-50.

	(1991, ¥2300)	20-35
BO9507	*Toho Special Effects Series #7-Godzilla vs. Mothra* (1992, ¥2500)	20-35
BO9508	*Toho Special Effects Series #8-Godzilla vs. MechaGodzilla* (1993, ¥2800)	25-40
BO9509	*Toho Special Effects Series #9-Godzilla vs. Space Godzilla* (1994, ¥2800)	25-40
BO9510	*Toho Special Effects Series #10-Godzilla vs. Destroyer* (1995, ¥2800)	25-40
BO9511	*Toho Special Effects Series #11-Mothra* (96, ¥2800)	25-40

Tokuma Communications
BO3401   *Godzilla Secret Technique Book* (Famicom) (1988, ¥400) $4-8

Tokuma Shoten
BO3501	*Daikaiju Bromide Zukan* (1979, ¥650)	$30-50
BO3502	*Godzilla vs. Mothra-TV Land Color Graph #52* (1992, ¥450)	6-12
BO3503	*Godzilla vs. MechaGodzilla-TV Land Color Graph #63* (1993, ¥480)	6-12
BO3504	*Godzilla vs. SpaceGodzilla-TV Land Color Graph #72* (1994, ¥480)	5-10
BO3505	*Godzilla vs. Destroyer-TV Land Color Graph #82* (1995, ¥480)	5-10
BO3506	*Godzilla vs. MechaGodzilla-TV Land Color Graph Deluxe Special* (1994, ¥950)	10-18
BO3507	*Godzilla vs. Destroyer-TV Land Book #55* (1995, ¥400)	5-10
BO3508	*Mothra-TV Land Book #67* (1996, ¥400)	4-8
BO3509	*100 Secrets of Godzilla-TV Land Color Graph Special #21* (1995, ¥400)	5-9
BO3510	*Super Visual Series-Godzilla* (1984, ¥980)	20-30

Town Mook
BO3551   *Visual Guide of First Godzilla* (1983, ¥780) $20-30

Uni Books
BO3601	*Art of Godzilla* (1991, ¥2800)	$30-50
BO3602	*Art of Godzilla vs. Mothra* (1992, ¥3000)	30-50

White Fang Project (MASH)
BO3701	*Godzilla Legend* (comic)(1987, ¥780)	$7-14
BO3702	*Godzilla Gaiden* (comic)(1994, ¥1000)	10-20
BO3703	*Godzilla Gaiden #2* (comic) (1995)	10-20
BO3704	*Making of Godzilla Legend* (comic)(1987, ¥500)	10-20

Yomiuri Shimbunsha
BO3801   *It's Godzilla* (1992, ¥480) $6-12

Yosensha
BO3901   *Monster Crazy-Way of a Godzilla Actor* (Hurricane Ryu story) (1996, ¥1300) $12-20

BOOKS –
U.S. Books
Random House

BO4001	*Godzilla, King of the Monsters (Ciencin)*	$3-5
BO4002	*Godzilla On Monster Island*	3-5
BO4003	*Godzilla Returns (Cerasini)*	4-7
BO4004	*Godzilla Saves America: A Monster Showdown in 3-D*	9-14
BO4005	*Godzilla vs. Gigan and the Smog Monster*	3-5

Miscellaneous Publishers

BO4101	*Godzilla (Ian Thorne)*	$40-60
BO4102	*Godzilla Book, The (Jim Harmon)*	12-18
BO4103	*Godzilla, King of the Monsters (Marrero)*	10-15
BO4104	*Illustrated Encyclopedia of Godzilla (Godziszewski)*	40-50

Coloring Books
Craft House (U.S.)

CR1001	*Godzilla Coloring Posters (1995)*	$6-10
CR1002	*Godzilla Coloring Pictures Box Set (1995)*	5-8

Resource Publishers (U.S.)

CR0630	*Godzilla King of the Monsters (1977)*	$30-40

Showa

CR2093	*Godzilla (1993)*	$5-8

Comic Books, Japanese
Inserted into Magazines

CB1001	*Destroy All Monsters (1968, Manga Oh)*	$70-120
CB1002	*Ghidrah, The Three Headed Monster (1965, Shonen Book)*	70-120
CB1003	*Godzilla (1955, Bokura)*	300-500
CB1004	*Godzilla (1954, Omoshiro Books)*	400-500
CB1005	*Godzilla (1954, Toho Tieup Advertising)*	400-500
CB1006	*Godzilla (1955, Shonen Club)*	500-600
CB1007	*Godzilla vs. The Sea Monster (1967, Bukun)*	150-200
CB1008	*Godzilla vs. The Sea Monster (1967, Toho Advertising)*	100-150
CB1009	*Last Godzilla, The (1957, Omoshiro Books)*	200-350
CB1010	*Monster Zero (1966, Shonen Book)*	70-120
CB1011	*Mothra vs. Godzilla (1964, Boken Oh)*	100-150
CB1012	*Revenge of Godzilla (1954, Shonen)*	400-500
CB1013	*Revenge of Godzilla (1955, Shonen Club)*	350-450
CB1014	*Son of Godzilla (1968, Shonen)*	80-100

Stand Alone

CB2001	*Godzilla (1958, Reimeisha)*	$250-400
CB2002	*Monster Godzilla (1954, Akashiya Shobo)*	500-700
CB2003	*New Godzilla (1958, Reimeisha)*	250-400
CB2004	*Revenge of Godzilla (1955, Akashiya Shobo)*	400-600

Stories in a Magazine

CB3001	"Godzilla vs. Gigan" (1972, Botsatsu Shonen Co.)	$50-70
CB3002	"Godzilla vs. Megalon" (1973, Monthly Shonen Champion)	40-60
CB3003	"Godzilla vs. MechaGodzilla" (1974, Monthly Shonen Champion)	40-60
CB3004	"Godzilla vs. The Smog Monster" (1971, Betsatsu Shonen Co.)	50-70
CB3005	"Son of Godzilla" (1968, Boken Oh)	70-100
CB3006	"Terror of MechaGodzilla" (1975, Monthly Shonen Champion)	30-50

Comic Books, U.S.
Marvel Comics

CB4001	*Godzilla*	#1	$6-10
CB4002/10	*Godzilla*	#2-10	ea. 3-6
CB4011/20	*Godzilla*	#11-20	ea. 2-4
CB4021/24	*Godzilla*	#21-24	ea. 3-6

Dark Horse

CB5010	*Dark Horse Comics*	#10	$3-5
CB5011	*Dark Horse Comics*	#11	3-5
CB5001/6	*Godzilla (1987)*	#1-6	ea. 4-8
CB5007	*Godzilla Color Special*	#1	5-9
CB5008	*Godzilla vs. Charles Barkley*	#1	3-5
CB5009	*Godzilla vs. Hero Zero*	#1	2-4
CB5101	*Godzilla*	#1	3-5
CB5102/10	*Godzilla*	#2-10	ea. 2-4
CB5111/16	*Godzilla*	#11-16	ea. 3-5

Fanzines
G-Fan

FA0001	#1	$20-25
FA0002/7	#2-7	ea. 15-20
FA0008/9	#8,9	ea. 8-12
FA0010	#10	20-25
FA0011/13	#11-13	6-8
FA0014	#14	10-15
FA0015/18	#15-18	6-8
FA0019	#19	8-10
FA0020/28	#20-present	4-6

Japanese Fantasy Film Journal

FA1001	#1	$40-60
FA1002	#2	25-40
FA1003/7	#3-7	20-30
FA1008/11	#8-11	15-20
FA1012/15	#12-15	8-15

Japanese Giants

FA2001	#1	$30-40
FA2002	#2	20-30
FA2003/6	#3-6	12-20
FA2007	#7	6-8
FA2008	#8	6-10

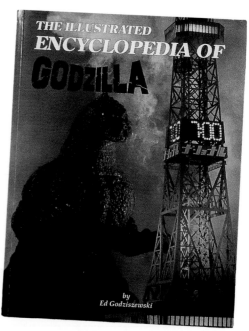

Above: BO4104 *Illustrated Encyclopedia of Godzilla* by Ed Godziszewski. $40-50.

Left: BO4002 and 4005 Godzilla Children's books. Each $3-5.

Assortment of Godzilla
Comic #1's. CB4001
(Marvel). $6-10. CB5001
(Dark Horse). $4-8. CB5101
(Dark Horse). $3-5.

Various issues of *G-Fan*
Magazine. Left to Right:
#7 $15-20. #9 $8-12. #14
$10-15. #25 $4-6.

Left: FA2004 *Japanese Giants*
#4. $12-20. FA2008 *Japanese
Giants* #8. $6-10. FA1014 *Japanese Fantasy Film Journal #14.*
$8-15. FA1013 *Japanese Fantasy
Film Journal #13.* $8-15.

Below: FA4114 *Famous Monsters*
#114. $40-70. FA5001 *Fangoria*
#1. $20-30.

Magazines –

Godzilla has appeared in countless magazines. It would take a whole book just to list all the articles he has been mentioned or appeared in. Most magazines with articles on Godzilla will run about $3-6. We have attempted to list some of the more famous and valuable ones here.

FA4114	*Famous Monsters* (c)	#114	$40-70
FA4135	*Famous Monsters* (c)	#135	10-15
FA5001	*Fangoria* (c)	#1	20-30
FA6013	*Fantastic Films* (c)	#13	6-10
FA8001	*Monsterland* (s)	#1	15-20
FA8002	*Monsterland*	#2	12-16
FA8003	*Monsterland* (c)	#3	8-12
FA9007	*Monster Times, The*	#7	8-12
FA9107	*Monster Times, The* (other issues, on cover of #'s 23,26,35,39,42)		ea. 6-10
FA2205	*Monsters of the Movies* (c)	#5	8-12

Novels

BN1001	*Godzilla* (Shigeru Kayama) (1954, Iwaya Shoten)	$1,200-1,800
BN1002	*Godzilla* (Shigeru Kayama) (1955, Shimamura Shuppan)	700-1,000
BN1003	*Godzilla/Revenge of Godzilla* (Shigeru Kayama) (1976, Kisotengai Sha)	30-40
BN1004	*Mothra vs. Godzilla* (X Books)	10-20
BN1005	*Godzilla vs. King Ghidrah* (X Books)	10-20
BN1006	*Godzilla* (X Books)	10-20

CALENDERS

Calenders have been made every year since at least 1972. The earliest ones were all artwork, later switching to paste-up photos. The ones since the mid-eighties have all been photo or poster artwork style.

CA1101 1967	$60-90
CA1001/4 1972-1975	ea. 50-80
CA1005/8 1976-1979	ea. 30-50
CA1009/13 1980-1984	ea. 20-40
CA1014/19 1985-1990	ea. 15-30
CA10020- 1991-present	ea. 10-20

CLOTHING & ACCESSORIES

Accessories

CL1001	Godzilla 1984 Shopping Bag	$8-15
CL1002	Godzilla vs. Mothra Tapestry	20-30
CL1003	Godzilla vs. SpaceGodzilla Shopping Bag	7-10
CL1004	Godzilla vs. SpaceGodzilla Tapestry	20-30
CL1005	Godzilla vs. SpaceGodzilla Umbrella	10-15
CL1006	Godzilland Shopping Bag (1984)	10-15

Adults

CL1101	G-Force Bomber Jacket (ltd. edition-400)	$300-500
CL1102	Godzilla Knit Sweater (lt. edition-250)	200-300
CL1103	Godzilla vs. Mothra Hooded Sweatshirt	40-60
CL1104	Godzilla vs. MechaGodzilla Hooded Sweatshirt	40-60
CL1105	Godzilla vs. MechaGodzilla Sweatshirt	40-60
CL1106	Godzilla vs. MechaGodzilla Bomber Jacket	450-550
CL1107	Godzilla vs. SpaceGodzilla Necktie	45-60

Children's

CL1201	Godzilla Stuffed Slippers (Bandai)	$15-25
CL1202	Godzilla Boxer Shorts (Ogran)	20-30
CL1203	Godzilla Socks (Ogran)	10-15
CL1204	Godzilla Tennis Shoes (Ogran)	30-40

Costumes/Masks

CL1301	Ben Cooper Halloween costume (1977)	$40-60
CL1302	Collegeville Godzilla Rubber Mask (1995)	15-25
CL1303	Takara Godzilla Plastic Mask (1991)	7-12
	Godzilla/King Ghidora pajama costume (Bandai, 1993)	
CL1304	adult Y7900	85-110
CL1305	child Y6900	75-100

Handkerchiefs

CL1401	Destroy All Monsters style (1977)	$20-30
CL1402	Godzilla vs. MechaGodzilla style (1977)	20-30
CL1402	Godzilla, King of the Monsters (1989)	10-15
CL1403	Godzilla Collage	7-10
CL1404	Godzilla vs. MechaGodzilla (1993)	7-10
CL1405	Godzilla vs. SpaceGodzilla	7-10
CL1406	Toho Monster Collage	7-10

Hats

CL1501	Godzilla Head-Shaped cap (Bandai, 1986)	$30-40
CL1502	Godzilla Silhouette ball cap (Toho, 1993)	20-30
CL1503	Godzilla SD Head ball cap (Concorde, 1995)	20-30
CL1504	G-Force ball cap (Concorde, 1995)	25-35
CL1505	G-Force Sabre design ball cap (Toho, 1994)	30-40

Key Chains

Bandai (pewter)

CL1601	Baragon, Godzilla (2 diff.), King Ghidora, Mothra (adult), and Rodan (2 diff.)	ea. $9-13

Godzilla Plate Time

CL1602	(All Godzilla vs.) Destroyer, King Ghidora, Mothra, and Space Godzilla	ea. $10-14

Lit-Godzi (Concord Paradise)

CL1603	Godzilla, King Ghidora, Little Godzilla, Mothra (adult), Rodan, and SpaceGodzilla	ea. $4-7

Swing Playing (Bandai, 1994)

CL1604	Godzilla, G-Force Mogera, Little Godzilla, SpaceGodzilla	ea. $8-10

Toho

CL1605	Godzilla vs. Destroyer CD Key-holder	$15-20
CL1606	Godzilla (Burning), Destroyer, Little Godzilla	ea. 7-10

Yutaka (pewter series)

CL1607	Godzilla, Destroyer, MechaGodzilla, SpaceGodzilla	ea. $9-13

CL1102 Godzilla knit sweater. $200-300.

CL1301 Ben Cooper Godzilla Halloween costume. MIB $40-60.

CL1603 LitGodzi key chains. Each $4-7.

CL1303 Godzilla plastic mask. $7-12. CL1302 Godzilla full head rubber mask. $15-25.

Lighters

Beetland
CL1608	Godzilla shaped lighter	$25-35

Groovy
CL1609	Godzilla plastic lighter (1995)	$6-10

Piezo
CL1610	Godzilla lighter (same as Beetland)	$22-32

Zippo
CL1611	Godzilla Lighter Collection (six lighters in set)	$160-200
CL1612	Burning Godzilla	80-120
CL1613	Destroyer	80-120

(The above two were a limited edition of 1,000 lighters, that when placed together formed a continuous scene).

Shoes

Banpresto Slippers
CL1701	Godzilla, King Ghidrah, Mothra, Rodan	ea. $15-20

Shirts

Concorde Plaza
CL1801	Godzilla vs. King Ghidora T-shirt	$25-30
CL1802	Godzilla vs. Mothra T-shirt	25-30
CL1803	Godzilla vs. MechaGodzilla T-shirt	25-30
CL1804	Godzilla vs. SpaceGodzilla T-shirt	25-30
CL1805	Godzilla vs. Destroyer T-shirt	25-30
CL1806	G-Force Polo shirt	40-55

General Products
CL1807	King Ghidora T-shirt	$25-30
CL1808	Godzilla T-shirt (3 different)	ea. 25-30

Sony Signatures
CL1809	Godzilla biting trains	$10-15
CL1810	Godzilla breathing fire 'all-over'	12-16
CL1811	Godzilla face 'all-over'	12-16
CL1812	Godzilla face w/planes	10-15
CL1813	Godzilla in city	10-15
CL1814	Godzilla w/Super X-II	10-15

Watches
CL1901	Capsule SD Godzilla Watch (1992)	$20-30
CL1902	Fossil limited edition w/pewter figure	150-200
CL1903	G-Force Watch (Toho, 1993)	45-75
CL1904	Godzilla 1984 Face	40-60
CL1905	Godzilla SD Watch (Yamakatsu)	60-90

CL1604 Swing Playing key chains. Each $8-10.

Left: CL1608 Godzilla shaped lighter. $25-35.

Below: CL1701 Banpresto slippers. Each pair $15-20.

CL1805 Godzilla vs. Destroyer T-shirt. $25-30.

CL1811 Godzilla giant face print T-shirt. $12-16.

COINS

CN1901	Godzilla Ariake Coliseum Exhibition Coin (ltd. to 5,000)	$9-16
CN1902	Godzilla vs. Mothra Coin	15-20
CN1903	Godzilla vs. MechaGodzilla Coin	12-18
CN1904	Godzilla vs. SpaceGodzilla Coin	12-16
CN1905	Godzilla vs. Destroyer Coin	10-15

COMPUTER ITEMS

Mouse Pads

CO1001	Godzilla 1954 poster	$15-22
CO1002	Godzilla (Godzilland, Yamakatsu)	15-22
CO1003	Godzilla foot shaped pad (Yamakatsu)	15-22
CO1004	King Ghidora (Godzilland, Yamakatsu)	15-22

Wrist Pads

CO1005	Godzilla (Yamakatsu)	$8-15
CO1006	King Ghidora (Yamakatsu)	8-15

Games

CO1101	Godzilla (1993),(Game for IBM)	$80-100
CO1102	Godzilla (1985),(NEC)	30-50

Screen Savers

CO1201	IBM (Impress Corp.)	$35-50
CO1202	Macintosh (Impress Corp.)	35-50

Software
Emotion

CO1301	Chronicles-Yuji Kaida CD-ROM Digital Gallery (1996)	$60-75

Imagineer

CO1302	Biology of Godzilla, The (1993), (Macintosh)	$40-50

Impress

CO1303	Godzilla Desktop Collection CD-ROM (Windows)	$30-40
CO1304	Godzilla Digital Gallery (1996), (Windows)	25-35
CO1305	Screen Saver for Macintosh (1994)	40-50
CO1306	Screen Saver for Windows (1994)	40-50
CO1307	Godzilla Collection, The	60-90

Music Mine

CO1308	Godzilla Digital Index (1995), (Macintosh & Windows)	100-130

Toho Digital

CO1309	Godzilla Movie Studio Tour (1996)	$90-120

CL1902 Fossil limited edition watch. $150-200.

CN1901 Godzilla Ariake Coliseum coin. $9-16.
CN1904 Godzilla vs. Space Godzilla coin. $12-16.

FI0561 *Ghidrah* 8mm film (50ft.). $8-12. FI0277 *Destroy All Monsters* 8mm film (200ft.). $15-20. FI1202 Godzilla talking View-Master reel. $15-25. FI0262 *Godzilla vs. The Thing* 8mm film (200 ft.). $15-20. FI1201 Godzilla View-Master reel. $12-20.

FILMS & VIDEO

Fuji Film

FI1001	Godzilla 1954 (1979)	$100-140

Ken Films

FI0229	Rodan, The Flying Monster (200ft)	$15-20
FI0236	Varan, The Unbelievable (200ft)	15-20
FI0261	Ghidrah, The Three Headed Monster (200ft)	15-20
FI0262	Godzilla vs. The Thing (200ft)	15-20
FI0263	Ghidrah Battles (200ft)	15-20
FI0277	Destroy All Monsters (200ft)	15-20
FI0278	Frankenstein Conquers The World (200ft)	15-20
FI0529	Rodan, The Flying Monster (50ft)	8-12
FI0536	Varan, The Unbelievable (50ft)	8-12
FI0561	Ghidrah, The Three Headed Monster (50ft)	8-12

FI0563	Ghidrah Battles (50ft)	8-12

G.A.F. Viewmaster

FI1201	Godzilla 'Godzilla's Rampage'	$12-20
FI1202	Godzilla, Talking Viewmaster	15-25

Sonosheet (Book and Film)

FI1301	Toho SFX Films Vol.1-8	ea. $50-70

Toho

FI1401	Mothra Attack Plan!	$40-60
FI1402	SFX Memorable Scenes (1975)	70-100

Cassette 8 Movies

FI1501	Godzilla vs. Ebirah	$20-30
FI1502	Minya's Battles	20-30
FI1503	Space Monster Ghidrah	20-30
FI1504	Violent Monster Battle	20-30

FOODSTUFFS

Candy

(Note: All prices here are for wrappers, not the food products)

FO1001	Godzilla Chocolate (Glico)	$4-8
FO1002	Godzilla Chocolate Snack (Morinaga)	2-4
FO1003	Godzilla Choco Snack w/puffy sticker (Glico, 1984)	6-9
FO1004	Godzilla Choco Snack w/card (Glico, 1992-94)	3-5
FO1005	Godzilla Gummi (Meiji, 8 diff.. packs)	2-4
FO1006	Godzilla Homerun	1-3

Other Items

FO1101	Corned Godzilla (Spam-style canned meat)	$6-12
FO1102	Godzilla American Corn (Brewery)	6-12
FO1201	Godzilla Cola (Brewery)	4-8
FO1301	Godzilla Gum (Meiji, 8 diff. packs)	4-7
FO1401	Godzilla Heads Gum (Amjrol, '88)	5-10
FO1501	Godzilla Homerun Cookies (Morinaga)	2-4
FO1601	Godzilla Lemon Gum (Glico)	2-4
FO1602	Godzilla Melon Drink	3-6
FO1701	Godzilla Popcorn (Brewery)	5-10
FO1801	Godzilla Ramen (noodle soup)	4-8
FO1901	Godzilla Stick Sausage (Yukijirushi Ham, '77)	8-12

Clockwise from top left: FO1201 Godzilla cola, $4-8. FO1701 Godzilla popcorn, $5-10. FO1801 Godzilla ramen (noodles), $4-8. FO1101 Corned Godzilla, $6-12. FO1501 Godzilla cookies, $2-4.

GAMES & PUZZLES

Card Games

GA1001	Godzilla Big Trump Card Game	$15-20
GA1002	Godzilla Card Game (Papel, 1992)	15-20
GA1003	Godzilla vs. Earth Defense Forces (Ten, 1992)	15-20

Card Games (Hiragana)

GA1004	Godzilla & Dinosaurs Karuta (Seika Note, 1975)	$20-40
GA1005	Godzilla Karuta (Showa Note, 1993)	8-15
GA1006	Godzilla Karuta (Suzuki Shuppan, 1965)	75-125

Children's Games

GA1101	Godzilla vs. Mothra Pachinko	$10-15
GA1102	Godzilla vs. Mothra Pachinko lg.	15-20
GA1103	Godzilla Slot Machine	15-20

Ideal

GA1151	Godzilla Game (1963)	$175-250

Mattel

GA1181	Godzilla Game (1977)	$25-40

Nomura

GA1201	Godzilla vs. Mothra Maze-Puzzle (1992)	$15-20

Takara

GA1301	Godzilla Fire Attack (1992)	$75-110
GA1302	Godzilla vs. MechaGodzilla Board Game (1993)	45-60

(comes with 3" plastic figures of Godzilla, MechaGodzilla 1993, plastic buildings and 3" rubber Rodan 1993 and Super XII, nice package)

Above: Left to Right: GA1103 Godzilla slot machine, $15-20. GA1101 Godzilla pachinko, $10-15. GA1201 Godzilla maze puzzle, $15-20. GA1102 Godzilla pachinko lg., $15-20.

Left: GA1151 Godzilla Game by Ideal. $175-250.

Role Playing Games

| GA1351 | Mothra vs. Godzilla Game for Adults (1982) | $25-40 |

Electronic Games

Bandai

GA1401	Godzilla Computer War Game (1984)	$40-50
GA1402	Godzilla Giant Monster Battle (1983)	30-40
GA1403	Godzilla Super BarCode Wars (1992)	12-16

Nintendo

GA1501	Godzilla, Monster of Monsters (Famicon, NES)	$20-25
GA1502	Godzilla 2 (NES)	20-25
GA1503	Godzilla (Gameboy)	20-25
GA1504	Godzilla's Adventure (Gameboy)	25-30
GA1505	SuperGodzilla (Super Famicon & SNES)	50-70
GA1506	Godzilla's Greatest Adventures (Super Famicon)	60-80

PC Engine/Turbo Duo

| GA1601 | Godzilla's Greatest Battles (Japanese version) | $80-100 |
| GA1602 | Godzilla's Greatest Battles (American version) | 70-90 |

Sega Saturn

| GA1651 | Godzilla Game | $60-80 |
| GA1652 | Godzilla (Game Gear) | 35-50 |

Takara

| GA1701 | Godzilla vs. MechaGodzilla Table War (LCD) | $25-40 |

Puzzles

APC (U.S.)

| GA1801 | Godzilla "King of the Creatures" (1978) | $20-25 |

Artbox

GA1901	Godzilla (Destroy all Monsters group photo)	$35-50
GA1902	Godzilla vs. King Ghidora	45-60
GA1903	Godzilla vs. MechaGodzilla 1993 (1000 pc.)	40-50
GA1904	Godzilla vs. MechaGodzilla 1993 (100 pc.)	8-15
GA1905	Godzilla vs. Destroyer	40-50
GA1906	Godzilla vs. SpaceGodzilla (1000 pc)	40-50
GA1907	Godzilla vs. SpaceGodzilla (100 pc)	8-15
GA1908	Godzilla (1954 style by bridge)	35-50
GA1909	Godzilla (movie posters)	45-60

Central Hobby

GA2001	Meltdown Godzilla	$45-60
GA2002	Burning Godzilla vs. Destroyer	45-60
GA2003	Fire Shooting (Godzilla)(2000 pieces)	45-80

HG Toys (U.S.)

GA2101	Godzilla "City Rampage"	$15-20
GA2102	Godzilla "Alien Attack"	15-20
GA2103	Godzilla "Air Attack"	15-20
GA2104	Bagged Set of all 3 w/posters	30-50
GA2468	Godzilla Giant Puzzle (14" x 36")	35-60

Seika

| GA2201 | Godzilla Puzzles (several different, 1970s) | $50-80 |

YanoMan Toys

| GA2301 | Godzilla (styles after '79 film festival poster) | $40-60 |

GA1301 Godzilla fire attack. $75-110.

Above: GA1302 Godzilla vs. MechaGodzilla board game. $45-60.)

Left: GA1351 Mothra vs. Godzilla game for adults. $25-40.

GA1602 Godzilla's Greatest Battles for Turbo Duo machine. $70-90. GA1503 Godzilla for Gameboy. $20-25. GA1502 Godzilla 2 for NES. $20-25. GA1651 Godzilla game for Sega. $60-80.

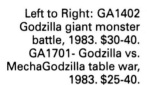

Left to Right: GA1402 Godzilla giant monster battle, 1983. $30-40. GA1701- Godzilla vs. MechaGodzilla table war, 1983. $25-40.

Left to Right: GA1903 Godzilla vs. MechaGodzilla puzzle. $40-50. GA1909 Godzilla posters puzzle. $45-60. GA1904 Godzilla vs. MechaGodzilla puzzle. $8-15. GA1902 Godzilla vs. King Ghidora puzzle. $45-60.

GA2201 Seika Godzilla puzzle. $50-80.

HOUSEHOLD ITEMS

Ceramics

HC1001	Godzilla Bank (figure)	sm. $10-15
		med. 15-20
		lg. 25-30
HC1101	Godzilla diorama ashtray (w/building)	12-16
HC1102	Godzilla diorama ashtray (w/city)	14-18
HC1103	Godzilla diorama ashtray (w/Mothra)	14-18
HC1104	Godzilla figural ashtray	14-18
HC1201	Godzilla figural mug	15-20
HC1105	Godzilla foot ashtray	10-15
HC1301	Godzilla Hatching from egg display	25-35
HC1401	Godzilla liquid dispenser	15-20
HC1501	Godzilla lotion dispenser	16-22
HC1601	Godzilla Sake set	10-15
HC1701	Godzilla Salt & Pepper shaker	16-22
HC1801	Godzilla Toothbrush Holder	14-18
HC1901	Godzilla Toothpick Holder	12-16

Drinking Cups

HD1001	Godzilla Drinking Cups (Game Prizes, 1996) (Godzilla, King Ghidora, Space Godzilla)	ea. $15-25
HD1002	Godzilla Drinking Glasses (Godzilland, set of two)	ea. 10-15
HD1101	Godzilla Drinking Mug, Bust (Concorde, 1995)	10-15
HD1102	Godzilla Drinking Mugs (Figural, Concorde, 1995) (Godzilla, King Ghidora, Little Godzilla, & Rodan)	ea. 10-15
HD2001	Godzilla Etched Glass Drinking Cups (set of two, Ifukube)	ea. 50-100
HD3001	Godzilla Hot/Cold Party Cup pack	2-4
HD1201	Godzilla vs. King Ghidora promotional mug (Toho, 1991)	20-30
HD1202	Godzilla vs. MechaGodzilla photo mugs (set of two, Toho, 1993)	ea. 10-15

Miscellaneous Items

HM1001	40th Anniversary Matchbook set (1994)	$30-50
HM1101	Godzilla Beach Towel, Matsui	18-26
HM1201	Godzilla Book Bag (General Products)	40-60
HM1301	Godzilla Bug Killer	15-20
HM3301	Godzilla Cereal Bowl (Concorde)	10-15
HM1401	Godzilla Clock (Yutaka, 1993)	30-40
HM1402	Godzilla/King Ghidora Clocks (Banpresto)	ea. 15-20
HM1403	Godzilla Clock (Konica)	10-20
HM1501	Godzilla CD Holder (Yutaka, 1993)	16-24
HM1601	Godzilla Curtain (Beetland 1983)	25-40
HM1602	Doorbell (Banpresto 1996)	12-18
HM1603	Godzilla Electric Shaver (Beetland, 1983)	30-50
HM1701	Godzilla Faucet Spinner (Yutaka, 1994)	10-16
HM1102	Godzilla Hand Towel (1989)	13-20
HM1801	Godzilla Ice Tray (1988, Beetland)	15-20
HM1802	Godzilla Shaped Ice Tray (Yutaka, 1993)	12-18
HM1901	Godzilla Lamp (Beetland, 1982)	150-225
HM1902	Godzilla Lunchbox (1991, metal)	30-50
HM2001	Godzilla Mini Vacuum	40-60
HM1103	Godzilla vs. Mothra Beach Towel (2 diff.)	ea. 25-40
HM2101	Godzilla vs. Mothra Lamp Cord (Yutaka, 1994)	10-15
HM1902	Godzilla Night Light (Gakken, 1984)	25-35
HM2201	Godzilla Pencil Can (1979)	20-30
HM2301	Godzilla Phone Rest (Bandai, 1984)	100-140
HM2401	Godzilla Pillows (1993)	sm. 14-20
		med. 20-30
		lg. 35-45
HM3302	Godzilla Ramen Bowl	10-15
HM2501	Godzilla Roaring Head Plaque (Funky Godzilla, 1984)	30-50
HM2601	Godzilla Scope (4 diff.. slide viewers)	ea. 12-20
HM2701	Godzilla Soap Dish (Yutaka, 1993)	14-22
HM2801	Swimming Pool- inflatable (Doussha, 1994)	40-60
HM2901	Godzilla Shampoo (Intl. Toiletries, '89)	12-20
HM3001	Godzilla Toothbrush Holder (Yutaka, 1993)	10-15
HM3101	Tissue Packs (Darei, 1994)	6-10
HM3201	Toilet Paper Holder, Roaring (Beetland, 1988)	50-75

Various Godzilla ashtrays, Left to Right: HC1101, $12-16. HC1104, $14-18. HC1105, $10-15. HC1102, $14-18.

HC1201 Godzilla figural mug, $15-20. HC1501 Godzilla lotion dispenser, $16-22.

HC1701 Godzilla salt and pepper shaker, $16-22. HC1901 Godzilla toothpick holder, $12-16.

HD1001 Godzilla drinking cups. Each $15-25.

Left: HC1601 Godzilla Sake set. $10-15. HD1202 Godzilla vs. MechaGodzilla photo mugs. Each $10-15. HD1102 Godzilla figural drinking mugs. (Left to Right: Godzilla, King Ghidora, and Rodan). Each $10-15.

Above: HD1002 Godzilla drinking glasses, $10-15. HM3302 Godzilla ramen bowl, $10-15. HD2001 Godzilla etched drinking glasses, each $50-100.

Above: HM1603 Godzilla electric shaver. $35-60.

Left: HM1901 Godzilla lamp (w/box). $150-225.

HM2701 Godzilla soap dish, $14-22. HM3001 Godzilla toothbrush holder, $10-15.

HM2801 swimming pool. $40-60.

INFLATABLES

Glico
IN1001	Godzilla 3" 'Bop Bag'	$5-10

Imperial Toys
IN1101	Godzilla 'Bop Bag' (48")	$15-20
IN1201	Godzilla inflatable (4 ft)	20-30
IN1202	Godzilla inflatable (6 ft)	40-50
IN1203	Godzilla inflatable (8 ft)	70-90
IN1204	Godzilla inflatable (12 ft)	125-150

TV Magazine
IN1301	Godzilla inflatable (15")	$20-25

LIMITED EDITION ITEMS

Concord Plaza (Lithographs)
LE1001	Burning Godzilla vs. Destroyer	$1,100-1,900
LE1002	Fire Shooting	1,000-1,800
LE1003	Godzilla Attack	1,000-1,800
LE1004	Godzilla Bay Bridge Carnival	1,800-2,500
LE1005	Godzilla Birthday in Manhattan	1,800-2,500
LE1006	Godzilla Forever	1,300-2,000
LE1007	Godzilla Monster Paradise	1,800-2,500
LE1008	Godzilla vs. Mothra Larva	1,000-1,800
LE1009	Howling Godzilla	1,300-2,000
LE1010	King Ghidora vs. Mothra	800-1,500
LE1011	Meltdown	1,300-2,000

IN1203 Godzilla 8ft. inflatable. $70-90.
IN1101 Godzilla 'bop bag'. $15-20.

LE1001 Burning Godzilla vs. Destroyer print. $1,100-1,900.

General Products
| LE1101 | Godzilla Bust, 1964 style (pewter, 1982) | $400-600 |

Hiruma Model Craft
LE1201	Godzilla in Crystal Ball (1995)	$250-300
LE1202	King Ghidrah in Crystal Ball (1995)	250-300
LE1203	Minya in Crystal Ball (1995)	150-200
LE1204	Rodan in Crystal Ball (1995)	275-325
LE1301	Atragon (60cm)	2,500-3,000
LE1302	P-1 Rocketship (55cm)	2,800-3,300

Kaiyodo
| LE1401 | Solid Silver Bust of Godzilla (9.5cm tall, 500g of silver, numbered edition of 300) | $1,800-2,200 |

Toho
LE1501	MechaGodzilla Prototype Casting (Toho)	$400-800
LE1502	Baby Godzilla Rod Puppet Casting (Toho)	600-1,000
LE1503	Godzilla vs. Mothra Staff Room Plaque (Toho)	100-200

Yuji Kaida Lithograph Series
| LE1601 | Godzilla | $1,000-1,800 |
| LE1602 | King Ghidora | 1,000-1,800 |

LE1101 Godzilla Bust. $400-600.

LE1201-1204 Crystal ball monster series. Left to Right: Minya, $150-200. Godzilla, $250-300, Rodan, $275-325. King Ghidora, $250-300.

LE1503 Godzilla vs. Mothra staff room plaque. $100-200.

MODEL KITS

Plastic

Aurora

		Built-up	Box only	MIB
MO1001	Godzilla (1964)	$40-60	$100-200	$300-450
MO1002	Glow-in the Dark Godzilla (1969)	20-30	40-60	150-200
MO1003	Glow-in the Dark Godzilla (1972)	20-30	30-50	100-150
MO1004	Godzilla's Go-Cart (1966)	500-1000	500-1000	3000+
MO1005	Ghidrah(1975)	75-125	100-150	250-350
MO1006	Rodan(1975)	75-125	100-150	250-350

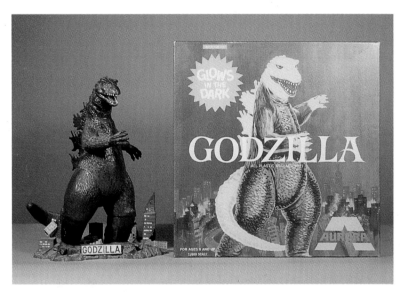

MO1002 Aurora glow in the dark Godzilla model, 1972. Assembled $20-30. MIB $100-150.

MO1001 Aurora Godzilla model, 1964. MIB $300-450.

MO1005 Aurora Ghidrah model kit, 1975. MIB $250-350.

MO1006 Aurora Rodan model kit, 1975. MIB $250-350.

Bandai

MO2001	Baragon Wind-up (1973)	$100-150	$30-50	$200-300
MO2002	Ghidrah Wind-up (1973)	125-175	30-50	225-300
MO2003	Godzilla Wind-up (1973)	125-175	30-50	225-300
MO2004	Mogera Wind-up (1973) never released			
MO2005	Mecha-Godzilla Wind-up (1974)	150-200	40-60	250-325
MO2006	Kaiju Series #11 Godzilla 1954			
	(1984)	15-25	5-15	45-65
MO2007	Kaiju Series MechaGodzilla (1984)	5-10	4-8	10-20
MO2008	Special Edition MechaGodzilla #13			
	(1992)	8-14	5-10	15-25
MO2009	Kaiju Series Godzilla 1964 (1984)	5-10	4-8	10-20
MO2010	Kaiju Series #8 King Ghidrah			
	(1984)	8-15	5-10	20-30
MO2011	Special Edition King Ghidrah #14			
	(1992)	12-18	7-12	25-35
MO2012	Kaiju Series #15 Godzilla 1954/93			
	(1992)	10-15	5-10	22-32
MO2013	Kaiju Series Super MechaGodzilla			
	#16 (1993)	12-18	5-10	25-35
MO2013	Byun Byun (go go) Series Godzilla			
	vs. King Ghidora (1992)	4-8	3-5	14-22
MO2014	Byun Byun (go go) Series Godzilla			
	vs. Battra (1992)	4-8	3-5	14-22
MO2015	Byun Byun (go go) Series Godzilla			
	vs. Mothra (1992)	4-8	3-5	14-22
MO2016	Godzilla SD (w/ Ghidrah) (parody)	4-8	4-8	10-15
MO2017	King Ghidrah SD (w/ Rodan)(parody)	4-8	4-8	10-15

MO2001 Bandai Baragon wind-up model, 1973. Assembled $100-150. MIB $200-300.

MO2006 Kaiju series #11 Godzilla. Bandai, 1984. MIB $45-65.
MO2012 Kaiju series #13 Godzilla. Bandai, 1992. MIB $22-32.

MO2009 Kaiju series Godzilla 1964 (with Mothra larva). Bandai, 1984. Assembled $5-10.

MO2015 and MO2013 Byun Byun models, Godzilla vs. Mothra and Godzilla vs. King Ghidora. Bandai, 1992. Each MIB $14-22.

MO2016 and 2017 Godzilla and King Ghidrah super deformed kits. MIB, Each $10-15.

Bullmark

MO3001	Godzilla, Remote Control (¥700, 1971)	$400-600	$200-400	$900-1500
MO3002	Godzilla, Wind-up (¥650, 1972)	300-500	175-350	800-1400
MO3004	Gigan, Wind-up (¥650, 1972)	400-600	200-400	900-1500
MO3005	Uni-puzzle Godzilla (¥50, 1972)	20-30	20-40	75-100
MO3006	Uni-puzzle MechaGodzilla (¥50, 1974)	25-30	25-45	90-120
MO3007	Uni-puzzle Gigan (¥50, 1972)	25-30	25-45	80-110
MO3008	Uni-puzzle King Ghidrah (¥50, 1972)	20-30	20-40	75-100
MO3009	Uni-puzzle Godzilla (giant size) (¥150, 1973)	30-40	5-10	60-80
MO3010	Uni-puzzle MechaGodzilla (giant size) (¥150, 1974)	30-40	5-10	60-80
MO3011	Uni-puzzle Ghidrah (giant size) (¥150, 1973)	40-80	5-10	90-125
MO3012	Wind-up Ghidrah (¥350, 1972)	40-70	30-40	150-200
MO3013	Toho Trio (set of 3 giant size figures) (¥700, 1974)	100-160	200-350	500-700

MO3002 Godzilla wind-up model. Bullmark, 1972. MIB $800-1400.

Boxes for Bullmark Uni-puzzles (MO3005-3008). Each $20-40.

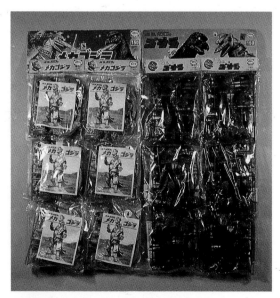

Display packs of Bullmark giant size uni-puzzle Godzilla and MechaGodzilla (MO3009-3010). Each pack $60-80.

MO3013 Toho Trio Bullmark model set (contains Godzilla, King Ghidrah and MechaGodzilla). MIB $200-350.

Marusan

The Marusan Plamodel series is the cream of the crop in Godzilla toys. The Plamodels are recognized the world over as the hardest to find and most valuable of the Godzilla toy series. To find one is quite an accomplishment, and to find one in a box is a very rare opportunity that the serious collector should not pass up.

MO4001	Plamodel Godzilla (¥380, 1964)	$800-1400	$1000-1500	$5000+*
MO4002	Plamodel Baragon (¥500, 1966)	900-1500	1000-1500	6000+*
MO4003	Plamodel Ebirah (¥650, 1966)	1200-1800	1500-2000	7000+*
MO4004	Plamodel Giant Godzilla (¥1200, 1967)	3000+	1500+	8000+*
MO4005	Plamodel Giant Gorilla (¥1200, 1967)	400-700	400-800	2000
MO4006	Plamodel Hatching Minya	700-1000	400-800	2000+*
MO4007	Moonlight SY-3 (¥250, 1968)	100-150	150-300	600-800

Misc. Plastic Kits

MO5001	Lindberg Godzilla (1995)	$3-6	$2-4	$8-12
MO5101	Monogram Godzilla (1978)	15-25	20-30	50-70
MO6001	Yamakatsu Godzilla (¥300, 1983)	5-10	5-10	20-30
MO6002	Yamakatsu Baragon (¥300, 1983)	5-10	5-10	20-30
MO6003	Yamakatsu MechaGodzilla (¥300, 1983)	5-10	5-10	20-30

MO4003 Ebirah Plamodel. Marusan, 1966. MIB $7,000+ .

MO4001 Marusan Plamodel Godzilla kit. MIB $5,000+

MO5001 Monogram Godzilla model. 1978. MIB $50-70

MO6001-6003
Yamakatsu Models;
Godzilla, Baragon
and MechaGodzilla.
1983. MIB $20-30.

Assembled
versions of
Yamakatsu
models
(MO6001-6003).
Each $5-10.

Garage Kits

Garage kits were first made in the early 1980s, as a response to adult collectors desires to build nice looking versions of their favorite characters. The first companies to make them did so literally out of their garages. As such, they do not usually come packaged in nice art boxes, but rather in plain cardboard boxes with glued on inserts. They also have not developed a large secondary market value. This is probably due to the fact that although they are heavily collected, they are not manufactured as collectibles. Garage kits are not bought by adults seeking to regain what they once had in childhood, but rather are purchased to assemble and paint. Many of the more popular kits are also reissued, helping to keep any secondary market value they might attain low. For these reasons, we are not listing any 'price guide' prices for garage kits, but rather are listing the original Japanese Yen price for them. In most cases you should be able to find (with some effort) any of the kits listed here. They will be priced anywhere from 20% under the Yen price up to double that price. Of course if the market changes, in future editions we will list collectors' prices on certain kits.

	Character	Metal/ Vinyl/ Resin/ Diorama	Size	Price
Aoshima				
MO0101	Godzilla	M	1/500	¥4800
MO0102	Gigan	M	1/500	¥4800
MO0103	King Ghidora	M	1/500	¥5800
MO0104	Mothra (adult)	M	1/500	¥4800
MO0105	Biollante	V	1/700	¥7000
Bandit				
MO0201	MechaGodzilla (1993)	V	1/400	¥7800
MO0202	Hedorah (flying)	V	1/250	¥4900
B-Club				
MO0301	Battra (adult)	R	1/500	¥18400
MO0302	Mothra (adult)	R	1/500	¥18400

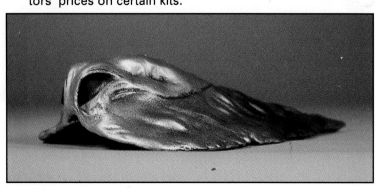

Above: MO0401 Godzilla (1962) vinyl kit by Billiken.

Left: MO0202 Hedorah resin kit by Bandit.

Far left: MO0403 Baragon vinyl kit by Billiken.

Left: MO0406 Godzilla (1965) vinyl kit by Billiken.

MO0408 MechaniKong vinyl kit by Billiken.

MO0503 Ebirah Vinyl kit by Falchion.

Billiken

MO0401	Godzilla (1962)	V	30cm	¥3000
MO0402	Godzilla (1964)	V	30cm	¥4000
MO0403	Baragon	V	30cm	¥3500
MO0404	Godzilla (1992)	V	30cm	¥6800
MO0405	Godzilla (1954)	V	28cm	¥4500
MO0406	Godzilla (1965)	V	1/150	¥4500
MO0407	Godzilla (1975)	V		
MO0408	MechaniKong	V		

Falchion

MO0501	Godzilla (1954)	V	50cm	¥12800
MO0502	Super-X2	V	1/50	¥3000
MO0503	Ebirah	V	36cm	¥4800
MO0504	Mothra (larva)	V	1/350	¥3500
MO0505	Maser Tank & Copter	R	1/150	¥9800
MO0506	Godzilla vs. Ebirah	V	1/150	

General Products

MO0601	Godzilla (1954)	M	10cm	¥4000
MO0602	MechaniKong	M	10cm	¥4000
MO0603	Baragon	M	10cm	¥4000
MO0604	Mogera	M	10cm	¥4000
MO0605	Baragon	V	50cm	¥18000
MO0606	Maser Tank	Paper	25cm	¥1500

Godzilla Shop

MO0701	MechaGodzilla (1993)	R	60cm	¥100000

G.O.N.G.

MO0801	Fire Rodan	R	1/500	¥4500

Horizon

MO0901	Godzilla	V	140cm	

Inoue Arts

MO1101	Godzilla (1964)	R	50cm	¥25000
MO1102	Baragon	R	50cm	¥25000
MO1103	Mothra (adult)	R	1/150	¥15000
MO1104	Mothra (larva)	R/D	1/150	¥20000
MO1105	Godzilla (1962)	R/D	1/150	¥28000
MO1106	Mothra vs. Godzilla	R/D	1/150	¥12000
MO1107	Atragon vs. Manda	R		¥35000
MO1108	Angilas (55 version)	R	50cm	¥25000
MO1109	MechaGodzilla 2	R	30cm	¥20000
MO1110	Planet X Saucer	R	10cm	¥2000
MO1111	King Kong vs. Godzilla	R/D	30cm	¥49800

MO0901 Godzilla pre-built
model by Horizon.

MO1101 Godzilla (1964)
resin kit by Inoue Arts.

MO1102 Baragon resin
kit by Inoue Arts.

Kaiyodo

MO1201	Godzilla (1954)	R	20cm	¥6800
MO1202	Godzilla (1955)	R	20cm	¥6800
MO1203	Godzilla (1962)	R	20cm	¥6800
MO1204	Godzilla (1964)	R	20cm	¥6800
MO1205	Godzilla (Son of ...)	R	20cm	¥6800
MO1206	Godzilla (1968)	R	20cm	¥6800
MO1207	Godzilla (1973)	R	20cm	¥6800
MO1208	Cybot Godzilla	R	25cm	¥8000
MO1209	Godzilla (1954)	R	40cm	¥12000
MO1210	Hedorah	R	10cm	¥4000
MO1211	Varan	R	10cm	¥4000
MO1212	Godzilla (1964)	R	40cm	¥12000
MO1213	Atragon	R	30cm	¥3000
MO1214	MechaniKong	R	20cm	¥4000
MO1215	Gigan	R	20cm	¥4000
MO1216	Gigan (flying)	R	20cm	¥3500
MO1217	Ghidrah	R	20cm	¥8000
MO1218	Minya	R	20cm	¥1800
MO1219	Rodan (1964)	R	20cm	¥4500
MO1220	Angilas (1968)	R	20cm	¥4500
MO1221	Baragon	R	20cm	¥4500
MO1222	Gorosaurus	R	20cm	¥4500
MO1223	Gorosaurus	R	30cm	¥15000
MO1224	Godzilla (1962)	R	25cm	¥7000
MO1225	Rodan	R	25cm	¥8000
MO1226	Godzilla (1954)	R	30cm	¥10000
MO1227	Baragon	R	30cm	¥10000
MO1228	Varan	R	30cm	¥10000
MO1229	Godzilla (1984)	R	15cm	¥4000
MO1230	Godzilla vs. Mothra (w/2 larvas)	R	10cm	¥6800
MO1231	Godzilla (1962)	R	SD	¥700
MO1232	Godzilla (1964)	R	SD	¥500
MO1233	Baragon	R	SD	¥500
MO1234	Godzilla (1968)	R	SD	¥500
MO1235	Angilas (1968)	R	SD	¥500
MO1236	Gorosaurus	R	SD	¥500
MO1237	Rodan	R	SD	¥500
MO1238	Varan	R	SD	¥500
MO1239	Manda	R	SD	¥500
MO1240	Minya & Mothra (larva)	R	SD	¥700
MO1241	Ghidrah	R	SD	¥1000
MO1242	Moonlight SY-3	R	SD	¥1000
MO1243	Ebirah	R	SD	¥500
MO1244	Kamakiras	R	SD	¥700
MO1245	Gabara	R	SD	¥500
MO1246	Kumonga	R	SD	¥1000
MO1247	Jet Jaguar	R	SD	¥500
MO1248	Megalon	R	SD	¥700
MO1249	Hedorah	R	SD	¥700
MO1250	Gigan	R	SD	¥700
MO1251	Godzilla (1989)	V	1m	¥97000
MO1252	Godzilla (1962)	V	1/100	¥18000
MO1253	Godzilla (1964)	V	1/100	¥18000
MO1254	Godzilla (1984)	R	30cm	¥4500
MO1255	Godzilla (1954)	V	20cm	¥3500
MO1256	Godzilla (1954)	R	25cm	¥18000

MO1257	Godzilla (1955)	V	20cm	¥3500
MO1258	Godzilla (1962)	V	20cm	¥3500
MO1259	Godzilla (1962)	R	26cm	¥18000
MO1260	Godzilla (1964)	V	20cm	¥3500
MO1261	Godzilla (1968)	V	20cm	¥3500
MO1262	Godzilla (1984)	V	20cm	¥3500
MO1263	Godzilla (1989)	V	1/400	¥4000
MO1264	Biollante	V	1/500	¥19800
MO1265	Godzilla (1991)	V	20cm	¥3900
MO1266	King Ghidora	R	1/350	¥12000
MO1267	MechaKing Ghidora	R	1/350	¥15000
MO1268	Godzilla (1992)	V	1/350	¥6800
MO1269	Battra (adult)	V	1/400	¥8800
MO1270	Battra (larva)	V	1/400	¥5800
MO1271	Mothra (larva)	V	1/400	¥1940
MO1272	Godzilla (1989)	V	SD 90mm	¥1500
MO1273	Mothra (larva)	V	SD 90mm	¥1800
MO1274	Godzilla (1992)	V	SD 90mm	¥1940
MO1275	Godzilla (1992)	V	SD 40mm	¥1500
MO1276	Mothra (larva w/egg)	V	SD 40mm	¥1500
MO1277	Battra (larva)	V	SD 40mm	¥800
MO1278	Godzilla (1954)	V	SD 40mm	¥500
MO1279	Godzilla (key chain)	V	SD 40mm	¥500

MO1201 Godzilla (1954) resin kit by Kaiyodo.

MO1225 Rodan resin kit by Kaiyodo.

MO1261 Godzilla (1968) vinyl kit by Kaiyodo.

MO1262 Godzilla (1984) vinyl kit by Kaiyodo.

MO1263 Godzilla (1989) vinyl kit by Kaiyodo.

MO1264 Biollante vinyl kit by Kaiyodo.

MO1268 Godzilla (1992) vinyl kit by Kaiyodo.

MO1291 Godzilla and Baby Godzilla super-deformed vinyls by Kaiyodo.

MO1257 and MO1281 Godzilla (1955) and Angilas vinyl kits by Kaiyodo.

MO1297 SpaceGodzilla resin kit by Kaiyodo.

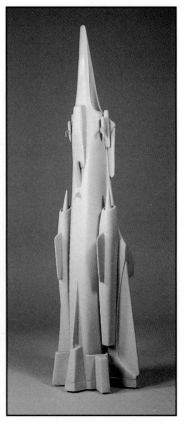

Moonlight SY-3 vinyl kit by Kaiyodo.

Godzillasaurus Resin kit by Kaiyodo.

MO1502 Godzilla (1962)
Head vinyl kit by M-1.

MO1280	King Ghidora (key chain)	V	SD 40mm	¥700
MO1281	Angilas (1955)	V	1/250	¥6800
MO1282	Super X (1 and 2)	V	1/250	¥1800
MO1283	Maser Tank	R	1/35	¥60000
MO1284	Maser Tank	V	1/35	¥25000
MO1285	Cosmos	R	1/1	¥7800
MO1286	Godzilla (1993)	V	1/400	¥4000
MO1287	Godzilla (1993)	R	1/400	¥15000
MO1288	MechaGodzilla (1993)	R	1/400	¥15000
MO1289	MechaGodzilla (1993)	V	1/400	¥4000
MO1290	Fire Rodan	R	1/400	¥16000
MO1291	Godzilla and Baby Godzilla	V	SD	¥2000
MO1292	MechaGodzilla (1993)	V	SD	¥1940
MO1293	Fire Rodan	V	SD	¥1800
MO1294	Godzilla (1994)	R	1/1000	¥8800
MO1295	Mogera (1994)	R	1/1000	¥8800
MO1296	Space Godzilla	R	1/1000	¥8800
MO1297	Space Godzilla	R	20cm	¥18000
MO1298	Godzilla (1994)	V	20cm	¥4000
MO1299	Little Godzilla (plaque)	R		¥25000
MO1300	Godzilla (1995)	V	20cm	¥4000
MO1301	Godzilla Jr.	R	15cm	¥8800
MO1302	Super XIII	R	1/200	¥7800
MO1302	Refrigerating Laser Tank	R	1/200	¥9800
MO1304	Destroyer (crab form)	R	20cm	¥18000
MO1305	King Ghidrah	R	1/250	¥28000
MO1306	Deformed Godzilla	R	15cm	¥15000
MO1307	Ghidrah Diorama	R/D	1/350	¥28000
	(includes Godzilla, Mothra, Rodan, and Ghidrah)			
MO1308	Godzilla against Mothra (adult)	R	1/350	¥7000
MO1309	Godzilla (1964)	R	15cm	¥8500
MO1310	Godzillasaurus	R	20cm	¥12000
MO1311	Moonlight SY-3	V	20cm	¥7000

Kotobukiya

MO1401	MechaGodzilla	R	1/350	¥25000
MO1402	Maser helicopter	R	1/72	¥12000
MO1403	Moonlight SY-3	R	1/350	¥12000

M-1

MO1501	Jumping Godzilla	V	1/250	¥4000
MO1502	Godzilla (1962) Head	V	1/1	¥19800
MO1503	Godzilla (1989) Head	V	1/1	¥30000
MO1504	Godzilla (1964)	R	50cm	¥82500
MO1505	Godzilla (1964)	V	50cm	¥23000
MO1506	Godzilla Skeleton (LTD/400)	V		¥35000
MO1507	Godzilla vs. Biollante	V/D	1/500	¥17000
MO1508	Godzilla & Nagoya Castle	V/D	1/350	¥15000
MO1509	Mothra vs. Godzilla	V/D	1/350	¥16000

MO1505 Godzilla (1964) vinyl kit (w/box) by M-1.

Max Factory

MO1601	Godzilla (1989)	V	27.8cm	¥5800
MO1602	Godzilla (1991)	V	27.8cm	¥6200
MO1603	Godzilla (1992)	V	21cm	¥5800
MO1604	Rodan (1956)	V	18.7cm	¥7200
MO1605	Mogera (1993)	V	20cm	¥5500
MO1606	MechaGodzilla (1993)	V	23cm	¥5800

Medicom

MO1701	Little Godzilla	V	1/4	¥12000

Pao

MO1801	Rodan (1993 Bust)	R	11.5cm	¥4800
MO1802	Manda II	R	48cm	¥6800
MO1803	King Ghidrah	R	1/500	¥26000
MO1804	Angilas (1955)	R	1/220	¥18000
MO1805	Godzilla (1955)	R	1/220	¥15000
MO1806	Godzilla (1964)	R	1/220	¥15000
MO1807	King Ghidrah	R	1/220	¥25000
MO1808	Mothra (larva)	R	1/220	¥3000
MO1809	Rodan (1964)	R	1/220	¥10000
MO1810	Base for above four kits	R	30 x 60cm	¥9000
MO1811	Destroyer	R	1/600	¥18000
MO1812	Baragon	R	1/220	¥15000

Paradise

MO1901	Godzilla (1954)	V	50cm	¥19800
MO1902	Baragon	V	50cm	¥19800
MO1903	Godzilla (1954)	V	30cm	¥6980
MO1904	Godzilla (1962)	V	30cm	¥6980
MO1905	Godzilla (1964)	V	30cm	¥6980
MO1906	Godzilla (1962)	V	60cm	¥19800
MO1907	Rodan (1956)	V	100cm	¥19800
MO1908	Mothra (larvas-2)	V	30cm	¥9800
MO1909	Godzilla (1989)	V	50cm	¥17800
MO1910	Mothra (adult)	V	70cm	¥12800
MO1911	King Kong swings Godzilla	V	20cm	¥12800
MO1912	Varan	V	60cm	¥19800
MO1913	Manda	V/D	1m	¥19800
MO1914	Godzilla swings Ebirah	V	30cm	¥19800
MO1915	Mothra bites Godzilla's tail	V/D	30cm	¥14800
MO1916	Mogera	V	30cm	¥17800
MO1917	Mecha-Godzilla 2	V	30cm	¥6980

RC Berg

MO2101	Godzilla (1954) mounted head	V	13cm	¥2500
MO2102	Godzilla (1962) mounted head	V	13cm	¥2500
MO2103	Godzilla (1964) mounted head	V	13cm	¥2500
MO2104	Godzilla (1989) mounted head	V	13cm	¥2500

Reds

MO2201	Godzilla (1962)	R	100mm	¥3000
MO2202	Godzilla (1964) (w/Mothra larvas)	R/D	100mm	¥5400
MO2203	Godzilla (1967) (w/Minya)	R/D	100mm	¥4800
MO2204	Godzilla against Ebirah	R/D	100mm	¥5400
MO2205	Godzilla (1954)	R/D	100mm	¥4800
MO2206	Godzilla vs. MechaGodzilla 1993	R/D	100mm	¥6500
MO2207	Fire Rodan	R	32cm	¥9800
MO2208	Godzilla (1993)	R	1/400	¥15000
MO2209	Little Godzilla	R	1/8	¥12000

Tsukuda

MO2301	Godzilla (1992)	V	35cm	¥8000
MO2302	MechaGodzilla1993	V	40cm	¥8000
MO2303	Godzilla (1993)	V	35cm	¥8000
MO2304	Godzilla (1994) (w/ little Godzilla)	V	30cm	¥8000
MO2305	G-Force Mogera	V	30cm	¥8000
MO2306	Space Godzilla	V	30cm	¥8000
MO2307	Destroyer	V	30cm	¥9800
MO2308	Godzilla (1995)	V	30cm	¥7800
MO2309	Godzilla (1964)	V	30cm	¥7800
MO2310	Rodan (1956)	V	1/160	¥5000

TVC-15

MO2401	Mothra Hatching (on temple rock)	R	20cm	¥5800

MO1602 Godzilla (1991) w/Godzillasaurus vinyl kit by Max Factory.

MO1606 MechaGodzilla (1993) vinyl kit by Max Factory.

Above: MO1911 King Kong swings Godzilla vinyl diorama kit by Paradise.

Lerft: MO1907 Rodan (1956) vinyl kit by Paradise.

MO1912 Varan vinyl kit by Paradise.

Wave

MO2501	Godzilla (1991)	V	21cm	¥15000
MO2502	Godzilla (1962)	M	50mm	¥1480
MO2503	Mothra (larvas w/egg)	M	50mm	¥1480
MO2504	Rodan (1956)	M/D	50mm	¥1480
MO2505	Baragon (vs. Frankenstein)	M	50mm	¥1480
MO2506	Hedorah	M/D	50mm	¥1480
MO2507	Varan	M	50mm	¥1480
MO2508	Gigan	M/D	50mm	¥1480
MO2509	Godzilla w/ Minya (1968)	M	50mm	¥1480
MO2510	King Caesar	M	50mm	¥1480
MO2511	Godzilla (w/Jet Jaguar)	M	50mm	¥1480
MO2512	King Ghidrah (1964)	M	50mm	¥1980
MO2513	MechaKing Ghidora	M	50mm	¥1980
MO2514	Biollante vs. Godzilla	M/D	50mm	¥1980
MO2515	Godzilla swings Ebirah	M/D	50mm	¥1980
MO2516	Godzilla vs. Super X	M/D	50mm	¥1480
MO2517	Anglias (1968)	M	50mm	¥1480
MO2518	Godzilla (1955)	M	50mm	¥1480
MO2519	Gorosaurus	M	50mm	¥1480
MO2520	Godzilla (1989)	M	50mm	¥1480
MO2521	Mothra vs. Godzilla	M	50mm	¥1480
MO2522	Anglias (1955)	M/D	50mm	¥1480
MO2523	Titanosaurus	M	50mm	¥1480
MO2524	Godzilla (1964)	M	50mm	¥1480
MO2525	Godzilla (1968)	M	50mm	¥1480

MO1913 Manda vinyl diorama kit by Paradise.

MO2526	Battra larva (w/Mothra larva)	M/D	50mm	¥1980
MO2527	Mothra ('92 adult)	M/D	50mm	¥1980
MO2528	Battra (adult w/ Godzilla tail)	M/D	50mm	¥1980
MO2529	Godzilla (1992)	M	50mm	¥1480
MO2530	MechaGodzilla (1974)	M/D	50mm	¥1480
MO2531	Megalon and Gigan	M	50mm	¥1980
MO2532	Gabara	M	50mm	¥1480
MO2533	Mogera	M	50mm	¥1480
MO2534	Kumonga and Kamakiras	M	50mm	¥1480
MO2535	Rodan (1964)	M	50mm	¥1480
MO2536	Little Godzilla	M	50mm	¥1480
MO2537	MechaGodzilla (1993)	M	50mm	¥1980
MO2538	Fire-Rodan	M/D	50mm	¥1980
MO2539	Godzilla (1993)	M/D	50mm	¥1980
MO2540	Gigan	V	30cm	¥6500
MO2541	Mothra (larvas w/egg)	V	30cm	¥2500
MO2542	Maser Tank	V	1/87	¥7800
MO2543	Godzilla (1962)	V	30cm	¥6500

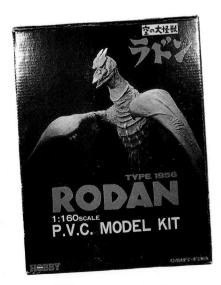

MO2310 Rodan vinyl kit by Tsukuda (in box).

MO2540 Gigan vinyl kit by Wave.

MO2543 Godzilla (1962) vinyl kit by Wave.

MO2730
Gabara
resin kit
by Volks.

MO2744
MechaGodzilla
(1974) vinyl
kit by Volks.

MO2702 Rodan
resin kit by Volks.

MO2731 Kamakiras and Kumonga resin kits by Volks.

Volks

MO2601	Godzilla (1964 type II)	R	1/144	¥15000	
MO2602	Godzilla (1989)	R	1/300	¥15000	
MO2603	Godzilla (1955)	R	1/144	¥14800	
MO2604	Godzilla (1991)	R	30cm	¥19800	
MO2605	King Ghidrah	R	30cm	¥39800	
MO2606	Godzilla (1962)	R	15cm	¥5800	
MO2607	Godzilla (1962 type II)	R	30cm	¥19800	
MO2608	Godzilla (1954)	R	15cm	¥5800	
MO2609	Godzilla (1954 type II)	R	30cm	¥16800	
MO2610	Godzilla (1992)	R	20cm	¥6800	
MO2611	Godzilla (1964)	R	30cm	¥16800	
MO2612	Varan	R	30cm		
MO2613	Godzilla (1993)	R	30cm	¥19800	
MO2614	Godzilla (1995)	R	30cm	¥16800	
MO2615	Little Godzilla	R	15cm	¥6800	
MO2616	Megalon	R	1/250		

Volks Cinema SFX Series

MO2701	War of the Gargantuas	R/D	1/350	¥4500	
MO2702	Rodan	R	1/350	¥8000	
MO2703	Angilas (1955)	R	1/350	¥5000	
MO2704	Ebirah	R	1/350	¥5000	
MO2705	Megalon	R	1/350	¥3800	
MO2706	King Caesar	R	1/350	¥3800	
MO2707	Hedorah	R	1/135	¥4800	
MO2708	Minilla	R	1/350	¥1200	
MO2709	Gigan	R	1/350	¥5200	
MO2710	Varan	R	1/350	¥4800	
MO2711	Godzilla (1966)	R	1/350	¥4200	
MO2712	Gorosaurus	R	1/350	¥4200	
MO2713	Godzilla (1955)	R	1/350	¥4800	
MO2714	Titanosaurus	R	1/350	¥3800	
MO2715	Godzilla (1984)	R	1/350	¥4200	
MO2716	Mothra (adult)	R	1/350	¥5500	
MO2717	Godzilla (1964)	R	1/350	¥4800	
MO2718	King Ghidrah	R	1/350	¥9800	
MO2719	Rodan & Mothra larva (1964)	R	1/330	¥4800	
MO2720	Godzilla (1989)	R	1/350	¥6800	
MO2721	Biollante	R	1/350	¥39800	
MO2722	MechaniKong	R	1/350	¥4800	
MO2723	MechaGodzilla	R	1/350	¥4800	
MO2724	Baragon	R	1/350	¥4800	
MO2725	Godzillasaurus	R	1/350	¥6800	
MO2726	Godzilla (1992)	R	1/350	¥7800	
MO2727	Godzilla (1966)	R	1/350	¥5800	
MO2728	Godzilla (1991)	R	1/350	¥7800	
MO2729	Bato-Godzilla vs. Mothra (larva)	R/D	1/350	¥8500	
MO2730	Gabara	R	1/350	¥4200	
MO2731	Kamakiras and Kumonga	R	1/350		
MO2732	Godzilla (1954)	R	15cm	¥5800	
MO2733	Godzilla (1993)	R	20cm	¥6800	
MO2734	SpaceGodzilla	R	20cm	¥9800	
MO2735	Godzilla (1994)	R	15cm	¥8800	
MO2736	Godzilla (1955)	R	16cm	¥6800	
MO2737	Angilas (1955)	R	15cm	¥6800	
MO2738	Godzilla (1964)	R	14cm	¥6800	
MO2739	Mothra (larvas w/ egg)	R	10cm	¥6800	
MO2740	Mothra (adult)	R	12cm	¥7800	
MO2741	Rodan (1956)	R	15cm	¥6800	
MO2742	Gigan	R	15cm	¥6800	
MO2743	Gorosaurus	R	15cm	¥6800	
MO2744	MechaGodzilla (1974)	V	30cm	¥6800	

Zokei-Kobo

MO2801	Appearance of Godzilla (1962) (Wonder Festival '95 exclusive)	R/D	1/250	¥19000	
MO2802	Appearance of Godzilla (1954)	R/D	1/250	¥10000	
MO2803	Godzilla (1964 bust)	R	1/100	¥25000	
MO2804	Godzilla (1984 bust)	R/D	20cm	¥25000	
MO2805	Appearance of Godzilla (1962) (Wonder Festival '96 exclusive)	R/D	1/250	¥18000	
MO2806	Original Image Godzilla (1995)	R	24cm	¥29000	
MO2807	Godzilla (1995)	R	20cm	¥15000	
MO2808	Godzilla (1964)	R	15cm	¥8500	
MO2809	Godzilla (1992)	R	20cm	¥15000	
MO2810	Godzilla (1962)	R	15cm	¥8500	

POSTERS

The poster section is divided into two categories, theatrical posters and commercial releases. The theatrical posters are listed in chronological order by popular American title with the Japanese title and release date in parenthesis. Price information for Japanese posters (as the country of origin), are always listed first. Next in line is the United States release title and information (if any), followed by any other countries release titles and information. Non-commercial posters that were produced as tie-ins for particular films are listed under that films' title. To expedite the listings of foreign posters, we have listed them by common equivalent American sizes, but their proper names and dimensions follow for your reference.

Argentina: 1 Sheet (29.25" x 43")
Australia 1 Sheet (27" x 41"), Insert (Daybill-13.5" x 30")
Belgium: 1 Sheet (14" x 21.5") or (16" x 22.5")
Czechoslovakia: (24" x 33")
Colombia: (19" x 27")
Cuba: 1 Sheet (27.25" x 36.5")
France: 1 Sheet (23" x 31") 2 Sheet (47" x 63")
Germany: 1 Sheet (23" x 33") Lobby Card (9.25" x 11.625") or (8.25" x 11.625")

Holland: 1 Sheet (27" x 41")
Italy: 1 Sheet (Affiso-39" x 55"), 2 Sheet (Double Affiso-55" x 79"), Insert (Locandina-13" x 27.5"), Lobby Card (Foto Busta-18" x 26"), Double Lobby Card (Double Foto Busta-26" x 36")
Japan: 1 Sheet (20.25" x 28.75") 2 Sheet Vertical 1954-1975 (22.75" x 65.5") 2 Sheet Vertical 1984-present (28.5" x 40.25"), 2 Sheet Horizontal (48" x 40") 3 Sheet (72" x 40"), Insert (Speed Poster-10" x 28.5"), International 1-Sheet 1954-1963 (20.25" x 28.5"), 1964-present (28.5" x 40.25"), Lobby Cards (11" x 14") or (10.25" x 14.5")
Mexico: 1 Sheet (24"x 35"), Half Sheet (15.25" x 19.75"), Lobby Cards (12.5" x 16.5") or (11" x 14.25")
Poland: (23" x 33")
Romania (22.5" x 32")
Spain: (27.5" x 39.5")
Sweden: (22.75" x 32.5")
Thailand: 1 Sheet (21.5" x 30.75")
United Kingdom: 1 Sheet (30" x 40") Lobby Card (Front of House Card-8" x 10")
United States: 1 Sheet (27" x 41"), 3 Sheet (41" x 81"), Half Sheet (22" x 28"), Insert (14" x 36"), Lobby Card (11" x 14"), Window Card (14" x 22"), 30" x 40" and 40" x 60" are self explanatory.

PO01001 Godzilla original Japanese one-sheet. Style A. $2,500-4,000.

PO01002 Godzilla original Japanese one-sheet. Style B. $2,000-3,500.

PO01101 Godzilla American
one-sheet. $600-1,000.

PO01105 Godzilla American
half-sheet. $300-600.

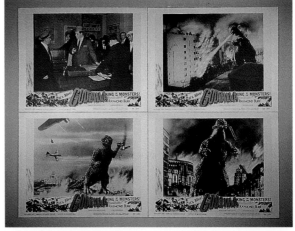

PO01107-01110 Godzilla American lobby card #'s 1-4. Each $30-150.

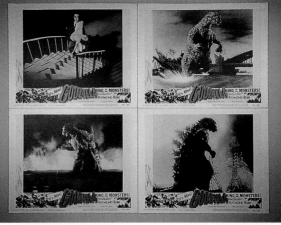

Left: PO01111-01114 Godzilla American lobby card #'s 5-8. Each $30-150.

Opposite: PO01020 Godzilla (American Version) Japanese one-sheet. $1,800-2,500.

Title	Country	Size	Price
GODZILLA			
(Godzilla, released November 3, 1954)			
PO01001 Gojira	Japanese	1 Sheet	$2500-4000*
PO01002		1 Sheet (Style B)	2000-3500*
PO01003		2 Sheet	3000-5000*
PO01004		2 Sheet (Vertical)	3000-5000*
PO01005		8 Sheet	10000+ *
PO01006		Insert (Vertical)	500-1,000*
PO01007		Insert (Horizontal)	1000-2000*
PO01008		1 Sheet 1977 re-release	30-50
PO01101 Godzilla, King of the Monsters (1956)	US	1 Sheet	600-1000
PO01102		3 Sheet	1000-1500
PO01103		40 x 60	700-1200
PO01104		Insert	300-600
PO01105		1/2 sheet	300-600
PO01106		24 Sheet	2000-3000*
PO01107/14		Lobby card	ea. 30-150
PO01020 Kaiju O Gojira (1957)	Japanese	1 Sheet	1800-2500*
PO01021		2 Sheet	1500-2500*
PO01021		Insert (Vertical)	400-800
PO01022		Insert (Horizontal)	300-700
PO01023 Godzilla, King of the Monsters	International	1 Sheet	700-1200
PO01201 Godzilla Rey De Los Monstrous	Argentina	1 Sheet	150-300
PO01206 Godzilla Roi Des Monstres	Belgium	1 Sheet	100-150
PO01211 Godzilla Rey De Los Monstrous	Cuba	1 Sheet	100-300
PO01216 Godzilla (1957)	France	1 Sheet	200-300
PO01217		2 Sheet	400-600
PO01221 Godzilla	Germany	1 Sheet	300-600
PO01226 Godzilla	Italy	1 Sheet	600-1000
PO01227		2 Sheet	800-1200

PO01228			Insert	300-600
PO01229/36			Lobby card	ea. 50-80
PO01241/8 Godzilla Rey De Los Monstrous	Mexico		Lobby card	ea. 30-40
PO01251 Godzilla (1957)	Poland		1 Sheet	500-700
PO01256 Godzilla	Romania		1 Sheet	300-600
PO01261 Japon Bajo-El Terror Del Monstruo	Spain		1 Sheet	400-500
PO01266 Godzilla Uhyrernes Konge	Sweden		1 Sheet	300-600
PO01271 Godzilla	UK		1 Sheet	300-500
PO01272/9			Lobby card	ea. 20-50

PO011201 Godzilla Argentine one-sheet. $150-300.

PO01206 Godzilla Belgium one-sheet. $100-150.

Above: PO011211 Godzilla Cuban one-sheet. $100-300.

Right: PO011217 Godzilla French two-sheet. $400-600.

PO01241-01244 Godzilla Mexican
lobby cards. Each $30-40.

PO1261 Godzilla
Spanish one-sheet.
$400-500.

PO01272-
01275 Godzilla
British lobby
cards. Each
$20-50.

PO01251 Godzilla Polish
one-sheet. $500-700.

PO01266 Godzilla Swedish
one-sheet. $300-600.

GIGANTIS, THE FIRE MONSTER
(Godzilla's Counterattack, released April 24, 1955)

PO02001	Gojira No GyakushuJapanese		1 Sheet	$2000-3000*
PO02002			1 Sheet (Style B)	1000-2000*
PO02003			2 Sheet Vertical	2000-3000*
PO02004			2 Sheet (Horizontal)	2200-3500*
PO02005			Insert (Horizontal)	800-1500*
PO02006	Godzilla Raids Again	International	1 Sheet	300-600
PO02101	Gigantis, the Fire Monster (1959)		US1 Sheet (Advance)	80-140
PO02102			1 Sheet	70-120
PO02103			Insert	50-75
PO02104			1/2 Sheet	50-75
PO02105			3 Sheet	100-150
PO02106			30 x 40	100-150
PO02107			6 Sheet	150-250
PO02108/15			Lobby card	ea. 20-40
PO02201	De Terugkeer Van Godzilla	Belgium	1 Sheet	40-80
PO02206	Le Retour De Godzilla (1957)	France	1 Sheet	100-200
PO02207			2 Sheet	150-300
PO02211	Godzilla Kehrt Zuruck	Germany	1 Sheet	150-300
PO02206	Il Re Dei Mostri	Italy	1 Sheet	150-300
PO02207			2 Sheet	200-350
PO02208			Insert	75-125
PO02209/16			Lobby card	ea. 40-70
PO02221/8	Gigantis, El Monster De Fuego	Mexico	Lobby card	ea. 25-35
PO02231	El Rey De Los Monstruos	Spain	1 Sheet	150-300

PO02001 Gigantis, The Fire Monster original Japanese one-sheet. Style A. $2,000-3,000.

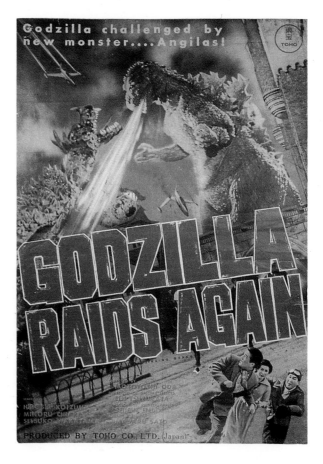

Above: PO02002 Gigantis, The Fire Monster original Japanese one-sheet. Style B. $1,000-2,000.

Right: PO02006 Godzilla Raids Again (alternate title for Gigantis, The Fire Monster) International style one-sheet. $300-600.

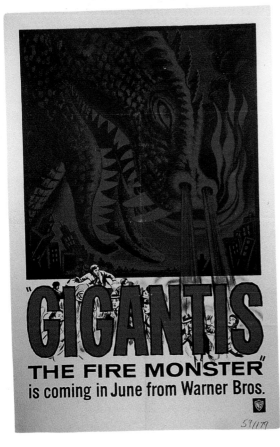

PO02101 Gigantis, The Fire Monster
American advance one-sheet. $80-140.

PO02102 Gigantis, The Fire Monster
American one-sheet. $70-120.

PO02108-02111 Gigantis, The Fire Monster
American lobby card #'s 1-4. Each $20-40.

PO02208
Gigantis Italian
insert. $75-125.

PO02221-0225 Gigantis Mexican
lobby cards. Each $25-35.

KING KONG VS. GODZILLA

(King Kong vs. Godzilla, released August 11, 1962)

PO03001	Kingu Kongu Tai Gojira	Japanese	1 Sheet	$600-1100
PO03002			1 Sheet (Style B)	550-1000
PO03003			2 Sheet	1000-1500
PO03004			3 Sheet	1200-2000
PO03005			12 Sheet	8,000+*
PO03006			Insert	250-400
PO03007		International	1 Sheet	300-500
PO03008/15			Lobby cards	ea. 50-100
PO03020		1964 release	1 Sheet	300-500
PO03920		reprint one-sheet		20-40
PO03025		1970 re-release	1 Sheet	60-100
PO03026			2 Sheet	80-120
PO03027			Insert	40-90
PO03028/35			Lobby cards	ea. 30-50
PO03040		1977 re-release	1 Sheet	30-50
PO03041/3			Lobby cards	ea. 25-40
PO03101	King Kong vs. Godzilla (1963)	US	1 Sheet	75-125
PO03102/3			40 x 60, 3 Sheet	ea. 100-200
PO03104/5			Insert, 1/2 Sheet	ea. 50-90
PO03106/13			Lobby cards	ea. 15-30
PO03201	King Kong vs. Godzilla	Australia	Insert	30-60
PO03206	King Kong Tegen Godzilla (1976)	Belgium	1 Sheet	30-50
PO03211	King Kong Contre Godzilla (1976)	France	1 Sheet	100-200
PO03212			1 Sheet (Style B)	80-150
PO03213			2 Sheet	200-400
PO03216	Rückkehr Des King Kong	Germany	1 Sheet	150-250
PO03217	Il Trionfo Di King Kong (1972)	Italy	1 Sheet	100-200
PO03218			2 Sheet	150-250
PO03219			Insert	75-150
PO03220/27			Lobby cards	ea. 30-70
PO03231/8	King Kong vs. Godzilla	Mexico	Lobby cards	ea. 20-30
PO03241	King Kong Contra Godzilla	Spain	1 Sheet	50-100
PO03246	King Kong vs. Godzilla	UK	1 Sheet	120-200
PO03251/8			Lobby cards	ea. 10-20

PO03001 King Kong vs. Godzilla original
Japanese one-sheet. Style A. $600-1,100.

PO03002 King Kong vs. Godzilla original
Japanese one-sheet. Style B. $550-1,000.

PO03020 King Kong vs. Godzilla 1964 re-release
Japanese one-sheet. $300-500.

PO03025 King Kong vs. Godzilla 1970 re-release
Japanese one-sheet. $60-100.

PO03041 King Kong vs. Godzilla 1977 re-release
Japanese lobby card. $25-40.

PO03040 King Kong vs. Godzilla 1977 re-release
Japanese one-sheet. $30-50.

PO03101 King Kong vs. Godzilla American one-sheet. $75-125.

Above: PO03106-03109 King Kong vs. Godzilla American lobby card #'s 5-8. Each 15-30.

Right: PO03206 King Kong vs. Godzilla Belgium one-sheet. $30-50.

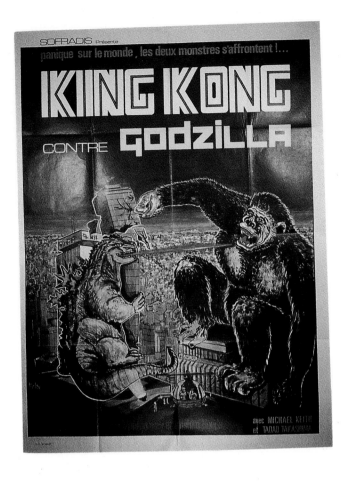

Left: PO03211 King Kong Contre Godzilla French one-sheet. Style B. $80-150.

Below: PO03231-03234 King Kong vs. Godzilla Mexican lobby cards. Each $20-30.

Above: PO03251-03254 King Kong vs. Godzilla British lobby cards Each $10-20.

Left: PO03241 King Kong vs. Godzilla Spanish one-sheet. $50-100.

GODZILLA VS. THE THING

(Mothra against Godzilla, released April 29, 1964)

Cat. No.	Title	Country	Format	Price
PO04001	Mosura tai Gojira	Japanese	1 Sheet	$300-550
PO04901			reprint one-sheet	20-40
PO04002			1 Sheet (Style B)	280-450
PO04003			2 Sheet (Vertical)	350-600
PO04004			3 Sheet	800-1400
PO04005			Insert	200-400
PO04006		International	1 Sheet	200-400
PO04007/14			Lobby cards	ea. 40-80
PO04020		1970 re-release	1 Sheet	60-100
PO04021			2 Sheet	80-120
PO04022			Insert	40-80
PO04023/30			Lobby cards	ea. 10-30
PO04040		1980 re-release	1 Sheet	30-50
PO04041			1 Sheet (Style B)	50-80
PO04042/9			Lobby cards	ea. 15-30
PO04101	Godzilla vs. The Thing (1964)	US	1 Sheet	75-100
PO04102			Insert	50-75
PO04103			1/2 Sheet	50-100
PO04104/5			40 x 60, 3 Sheet	ea. 100-175
PO04106/13			Lobby cards	ea. 15-30
PO04201	Godzilla Affronte La Chose (1971)	Belgium	1 Sheet	30-50
PO04206	Godzilla Und Die Urweltraupen	Germany	1 Sheet	20-40
PO04207/16			Lobby cards	ea. 5-15
PO04226	Godzilla En Het Monster Van Mothra	Holland	1 Sheet	50-100
PO04231	Watang! Nel Favoloso Impero Dei Mostri	Italy	1 Sheet	100-200
PO04232			2 Sheet	150-250
PO04233			Insert	75-150
PO04234/41			Lobby cards	ea. 30-60
PO04246/53	Godzilla Contre Mothra	Mexico	Lobby cards	ea. 20-30
PO04256	Godzilla Contre Los Monstrous	Spain	1 Sheet	30-60
PO04261	Godzilla vs. The Thing	UK	1 Sheet	100-200
PO04262/9			Lobby cards	ea. 10-20
PO04276		re-release	1 Sheet	30-60

PO04001 Godzilla vs. the Thing original Japanese one-sheet. Style A. $300-550.

Above: PO04002 Godzilla vs. the Thing original Japanese one-sheet. Style B. $280-450.

Right: PO04020 Godzilla vs. the Thing 1970 re-release Japanese one-sheet. $60-110.

PO04040 Godzilla vs. the Thing 1980 re-release
Japanese one-sheet. Style A. $30-50.

PO04101 Godzilla vs. the Thing
American one-sheet. $75-100.

PO04103 Godzilla vs. the Thing
American half-sheet. $50-100.

PO04106-04109 Godzilla vs. the Thing
American lobby card #'s 1-4. Each $15-30.

PO04206 Godzilla vs. the Thing
German one-sheet. $20-40.

PO04207-04210 Godzilla vs. the Thing
German lobby cards. Each $5-15.

PO04246 Godzilla vs. the Thing
Mexican lobby card. $20-30.

PO04231 Godzilla vs. the Thing
Italian one-sheet. $100-200.

PO04262-04265 Godzilla vs. the Thing
British lobby cards. Each $10-20.

GHIDRAH, THE THREE HEADED MONSTER

(Three Giant Monsters-Earth's Greatest Decisive Battle, released December 20, 1964)

PO05001	San Daikaiju-Chikyu Saidai No Kessen	Japanese	1 Sheet	$250-450
PO05901			reprint one-sheet	20-40
PO05002			1 Sheet (Style B)	220-400
PO05003			2 Sheet (Vertical)	300-550
PO05004			3 Sheet	500-1000
PO05005			Insert	125-250
PO05006		International	1 Sheet	200-350
PO05007/14			Lobby cards	ea. 30-60
PO05020	Gojira, Mosura, Kingu Gidora-Chikyu Saidai No Kessen	1971 re-release	1 Sheet	50-90
PO05021			2 Sheet	80-120
PO05022			Insert	40-80
PO05023/30			Lobby cards	ea. 10-40
PO05101	Ghidrah, The Three Headed Monster (1965)	US	1 Sheet	50-75
PO05102			1 Sheet (Military style)	30-60
PO05103/4			1/2 Sheet, Insert	ea. 30-50
PO05105/6			40 x 60, 3 Sheet	ea. 75-125
PO05107/14			Lobby cards	ea. 10-20
PO05201/8	Ghidra, Monstruo De 3 Cabazas	Mexico	Lobby cards	ea. 15-20
PO05211	Ghidra, Monstruo De 3 Cabazas	Spain	1 Sheet	50-100

PO05001 Ghidrah original Japanese one-sheet. Style A. $250-450.

PO05002 Ghidrah original Japanese one-sheet. Style B. $220-400.

PO05020 Ghidrah 1971 re-release
Japanese one-sheet. $50-90.

PO05023-05026 Ghidrah 1971 re-release
Japanese lobby cards. Each $10-40.

PO05101 Ghidrah
American one-sheet.
$50-75

PO0511-05114 Ghidrah American
lobby card #'s 1-4. Each $10-20.

PO05201-5202 Ghidrah Mexican
lobby cards. Each $15-25.

PO05103
Ghidrah
American
half-sheet.
$30-50.

PO06001 Monster Zero original Japanese one-sheet. Style A. $225-425.

PO06002 Monster Zero original Japanese one-sheet. Style B. $200-400.

PO06007 Monster Zero original Japanese lobby card. $25-50.

MONSTER ZERO

(Great Monster War, released December 19, 1965)

PO06001	Kaiju Daisenso	Japanese	1 Sheet	$225-425
PO06002			1 Sheet (Style B)	200-400
PO06003			2 Sheet (Vertical)	250-500
PO06004			3 Sheet	500-1000
PO06005			Insert	125-250
PO06006		International	1 Sheet	100-200
PO06007/14			Lobby cards	ea. 25-50
PO06020	Kaiju Daisenso-Kingu Gidora tai Gojira	1971 re-release		50-90
PO06021			2 Sheet	80-120
PO06022			Insert	40-80
PO06023/30			Lobby cards	ea. 20-40
PO06101	Monster Zero (1970)	US	1 Sheet (combo)	40-60
PO06102			1/2 Sheet	30-50
PO06103/4			Lobby cards	ea. 20-30
PO06105	Invasion of the Astros	US	1 Sheet (alt.)	50-80
PO06201	Invasion Planeet X	Belgium	1 Sheet	30-50

PO06020 Monster Zero 1971 re-release Japanese one-sheet. $50-90.

PO06023 Monster Zero 1971
re-release lobby card. $20-40.

PO06101 Monster Zero/War of the
Gargantuas American one-sheet. $40-60.

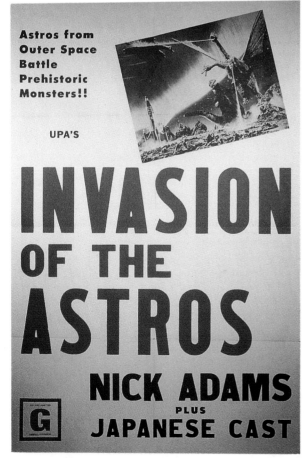

PO06105 Invasion of the Astros
American one-sheet. $50-80.

PO06103-06104 Monster Zero American
lobby cards. Each $20-30.

PO06206	La Invasion Del Astro-Monstruo	Colombia	1 Sheet	30-50
PO06211	Útok Z Neznáma	Czechoslovakia	1 Sheet	150-250
PO06216	Invasion Planete X (1967)	France	1 Sheet	60-100
PO06217			2 Sheet	80-150
PO06221	Befehl Aus Dem Dunkel	Germany	1 Sheet	30-60
PO06231	Anno 2000 L'Invasione Degli Astro Mostri	Italy	1 Sheet	80-140
PO06232			2 Sheet	125-200
PO06233			Insert	60-100
PO06234/40			Lobby cards	ea. 30-50
PO06251/8	La Invasion De Los Astro-Monstruos	Mexico	Lobby cards	ea. 15-25
PO06261		Poland	1 Sheet	200-300
PO06266	Los Monstruos Invaden La Tierra	Spain	1 Sheet	50-100
PO06271		Taiwan	1 Sheet	25-50

PO06201 Monster Zero
Belgium one-sheet. $30-50.

PO06206 Monster Zero
Colombian one-sheet. $30-50.

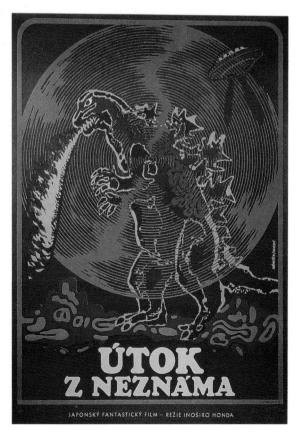

PO06211 Monster Zero Czechoslovakia
one-sheet. $150-250.

PO06251-06252 Monster Zero
Mexican lobby cards. Each $15-25.

GODZILLA VS. THE SEA MONSTER

(Godzilla, Ebirah, Mothra-Great Duel in the South Seas, released December 17, 1966)

PO07001	Gojira, Ebira, Mosura-Nakano No Daiketto	Japanese	1 Sheet	$175-350
PO07002			1 Sheet (Style B)	160-325
PO07003			2 Sheet (Vertical)	200-400
PO07004			3 Sheet	500-1000
PO07005			Insert	125-225
PO07006			1 Sheet (Marusan tie-in)	150-300
PO07007		International	1 Sheet	100-200
PO07008/15			Lobby cards	ea. 25-50
PO07020		1972 re-release	1 Sheet	40-80
PO07021			2 Sheet	80-120
PO07022			Insert	35-70
PO07023/30			Lobby cards	ea. 10-40
PO07201	Ebirah Horror en las profundidades!	Colombia	1 Sheet	30-50
PO07206	Ebirah Contre Godzilla (1981)	France	1 Sheet	60-100
PO07207			2 Sheet	75-150
PO07211	Frankenstein Und Die Ungeheuer Aus Dem Meer	Germany	1 Sheet	25-50
PO07212/23			Lobby cards	ea. 5-10
PO07231	Ebirah-Horror of the Deep	Holland	1 Sheet	60-100
PO07236	Il Ritorno Di Godzilla	Italy	1 Sheet	75-125
PO07237			2 Sheet	100-150
PO07238			Insert	50-90
PO07239/46			Lobby cards	ea. 20-50
PO07252/9	Ebirah Terror De Los Mares vs. Godzilla	Mexico	Lobby cards	ea. 15-20
PO07260	Godzilla Contra Terror De Los Mares (re-release)	Mexico	1/2 Sheet	25-40
PO07261/8	Godzilla Contra Terror De Los Mares (re-release)	Mexico	Lobby cards	ea.12-20
PO07271	Ebirah-Potwor Z Gtebin	Poland	1 Sheet	100-200
PO07276	Los Monstrous Del Mar	Spain	1 Sheet	50-100

PO07001 Godzilla vs. the Sea Monster original Japanese one-sheet. Style A. $175-350.

PO07002 Godzilla vs. the Sea Monster original Japanese one-sheet. Style B. $160-325.

PO07008-07009 Godzilla vs. the Sea Monster Japanese lobby cards. Each $25-50.

PO07020 Godzilla vs. the Sea Monster 1972 re-release Japanese one-sheet. $40-80.

PO07007 Godzilla vs. the Sea Monster International one-sheet. $100-200.

PO07239 Godzilla vs. the Sea Monster Italian lobby card. $20-50.

PO07236 Godzilla vs. the Sea Monster Italian one-sheet. $75-125.

PO07260 Godzilla vs. the Sea Monster Mexican re-release half-sheet. $25-40.

PO07271 Godzilla vs. the Sea Monster Polish one-sheet. $100-200.

SON OF GODZILLA

(Decisive Battle on Monster Island, Son of Godzilla, released December 16, 1967)

PO08001	Kaiju Shima No Kessen-Gojira No Musuko	Japanese	1 Sheet	$100-250
PO08002			1 Sheet (Style B)	100-250
PO08003			2 Sheet (Vertical)	175-350
PO08004			3 Sheet	400-700
PO08005			Insert	100-200
PO08006			1 Sheet Marusan	100-200
PO08007		International	1 Sheet	75-125
PO08008/15			Lobby cards	ea. 20-60
PO08020		1973 re-release	1 Sheet	40-80
PO08021			2 Sheet	70-100
PO08022			Insert	30-70
PO08023/30			Lobby cards	ea. 10-30

PO08201	Le Planete Des Monstres (1978)	Belgium	1 Sheet	20-40
PO08206		Egypt	1 Sheet	50-100
PO08211	La Planete Des Monstres	France	1 Sheet	40-80
PO08212			2 Sheet	60-100
PO08216	Frankensteins Monster Jagen Godzilla's Sohn	Germany	1 Sheet	30-60
PO08217/28			Lobby cards	ea. 5-10
PO08241	Il Figlio Di Godzilla (1969)	Italy	1 Sheet	60-120
PO08242			2 Sheet	100-150
PO08243			Insert	40-80
PO08244/51			Lobby cards	ea. 20-50
PO08261/8	El Hijo De Godzilla	Mexico	Lobby cards	ea. 10-20
PO08271	Syn Godzilla	Poland	1 Sheet	100-200
PO08276	El Hijo De Godzilla	Spain	1 Sheet	60-100

PO08001 Son of Godzilla original
Japanese one-sheet. Style A. $100-250.

PO08007 Son of Godzilla International
one-sheet. $75-125

PO08020 Son of Godzilla 1973 re-release
Japanese one-sheet. $40-80.

PO08008 Son of Godzilla Japanese lobby card. $20-60.
PO08023 Son of Godzilla re-release Japanese lobby card. $10-30.

PO08211 Son of Godzilla French two-sheet. $60-100.

PO08216 Son of Godzilla German one-sheet. $30-60.

PO08242 Son of Godzilla Italian two-sheet. $100-150.

PO08243 Son of Godzilla Italian insert. $40-80.

PO08276 Son of Godzilla Spanish one-sheet. $60-100.

DESTROY ALL MONSTERS

(Monsters All Attack, released August 1, 1968)

PO09001	Kaiju Soshingeki	Japanese	1 Sheet	$150-250
PO09002			2 Sheet (Vertical)	200-400
PO09003			3 Sheet	400-800
PO09004			Insert	50-100
PO09005			1 Sheet (Marusan)	100-200
PO09006		International	1 Sheet	125-200
PO09007/14			Lobby cards	ea. 20-60
PO09020	Gojira's Dengeki			
	Daisakusen	1973 re-release	1 Sheet	75-150
PO09021			3 Sheet	90-70
PO09022			Insert	40 -80
PO09023/30			Lobby cards	ea. 10-40
PO09101	Destroy All			
	Monsters (1969)	US	1 Sheet	45-90
PO09102			30 x 40	50-100
PO09103/4			Insert, 1/2 Sheet	ea. 30-60
PO09105/12			Lobby cards	ea. 10-20
PO09201	Les Envahisseurs			
	Attaquent (1970)	Belgium	1 Sheet	30-50
PO09206	Les Envahisseurs			
	Attaquent (1970)	France	1 Sheet	50-100
PO09207			2 Sheet	100-200
PO09208			2 Sheet (Style B)	50-100
PO09216	Frankenstein Und			
	Die Monster			
	Aus Dem All	Germany	1 Sheet	40-80
PO09217/27			Lobby cards	ea. 10-20
PO09241	Gli Eredi Di King Kong	Italy	1 Sheet	70-120
PO09242			2 Sheet	100-200
PO09243			Insert	40-80
PO09244/51			Lobby cards	ea. 40-70
PO09252			'Double' Lobby card	80-120
PO09261/8	Los Monstruos			
	Invaden La Tierra	Mexico	Lobby cards	ea. 15-25
PO09271	Destroy All Monsters	UK	1 Sheet	100-200
PO09272/9			Lobby cards	ea. 15-25

PO09001 Destroy All Monsters original
Japanese one-sheet. $150-250.

PO09007 Destroy All Monsters
original Japanese lobby card.

PO09020 Destroy All Monsters 1973
re-release Japanese poster. $75-150.

PO09020 Destroy All Monsters
International one-sheet. $125-200.

PO09101
Destroy All
Monsters
American one-
sheet. $45-90.

Above: PO09105-09108 Destroy All Monsters
American lobby card #'s 1-4. Each $10-20.

Right: PO09207 Destroy All Monsters French
two-sheet. Style A. $100-200.

PO09208 Destroy All
Monsters French
two-sheet. Style B.
$50-100.

Right: PO09216
Destroy All Monsters
German one-sheet.
$40-80.

Far right: PO09244
Destroy All Monsters
Italian lobby card.
$40-70.

Above: PO09252 Destroy All Monsters Italian double lobby card. $80-120.

Right: PO09261-09264 Destroy All Monsters Mexican lobby cards. Each $15-25.

GODZILLA'S REVENGE

(Godzilla, Minya, Gabara-All Monsters Attack, released December 20, 1969)

PO10001	Gojira, Minira, Gabara-Oru Kaiju Daishingeki	Japanese	1 Sheet	$75-150
PO10002			2 Sheet (Vertical)	100-200
PO10003			Insert	50-100
PO10004			1 Sheet (map)	60-120
PO10005		International	1 Sheet	50-100
PO10006/13			Lobby cards	ea. 15-30
PO10101	Godzilla's Revenge (1969)	US	1 Sheet (combo)	30-60
PO10102	Minya, Son of Godzilla (1969)	US	1 Sheet	40-80
PO10201		France	1 Sheet	75-125
PO10206	La Vendetta Di Godzilla	Italy	1 Sheet	40-80
PO10207			2 Sheet	60-100
PO10208			Insert	30-60
PO10209/16			Lobby cards	ea. 20-40

PO10001 Godzilla's Revenge Japanese one-sheet. $75-150.

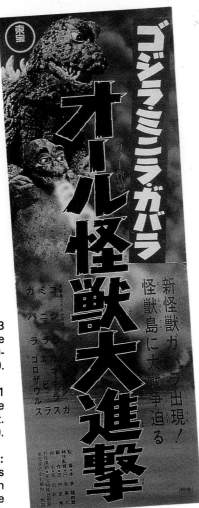

Right: PO10003 Godzilla's Revenge Japanese insert. $50-100.

Below left: PO10101 Godzilla's Revenge American one-sheet. $30-60.

Below right: PO10102 Godzilla's Revenge American one-sheet (alternate title). $40-80.

PO10006-10008 Godzilla's Revenge Japanese lobby cards. Each $15-30.

GODZILLA VS. THE SMOG MONSTER

(Godzilla vs. Hedorah, released July 24, 1971)

PO11001	Gojira Tai Hedora	Japanese	1 Sheet	$60-100
PO11002			2 Sheet (Vertical)	80-150
PO11003			Insert	50-90
PO11004			2 Sheet (Hedora Diagram)	100-200
PO11005		International	1 Sheet	75-125
PO11006/13			Lobby cards	ea. 15-30
PO11101	Godzilla vs. The Smog Monster (1972)	US	1 Sheet	30-50
PO11102			30 x 40	40-80
PO11103/10			Lobby cards	ea. 5-15
PO11201	Godzilla Contre Le Monstre Du Brouillard	Belgium	1 Sheet	15-30
PO11206		France	1 Sheet	60-100
PO11207			2 Sheet	75-125
PO11211	Frankenstein's Kampf Gegen Die Teufel Monster (1972)	Germany	1 Sheet	20-30
PO11212/27			Lobby cards	ea. 5-15
PO11241	Godzilla-Furia Di Mostri	Italy	1 Sheet	60-100
PO11242			2 Sheet	80-130
PO11243			Insert	30-60
PO11244/51			Lobby cards	ea. 20-40
PO11261/68	Los Monstrous Del Smog	Mexico	Lobby cards	ea. 10-20
PO11276	Godzilla Kontra Hedora	Poland	1 Sheet	75-125

PO11001 Godzilla vs. The Smog Monster Japanese one-sheet. $60-100.

PO11004 Godzilla vs. The Smog Monster Japanese two-sheet. $100-200.

PO11005
Godzilla vs.
The Smog
Monster
International
one-sheet.
$75-125.

PO11006-11008 Godzilla vs. The
Smog Monster Japanese lobby
cards. Each $15-30.

Above: PO11103-11105 Godzilla vs.
The Smog Monster American lobby
card #'s 1-4. Each $5-15.

Left: PO11101 Godzilla vs. The Smog
Monster American one-sheet. $30-50.

PO11211 Godzilla vs. The Smog Monster German one-sheet. $20-30.

Above: PO11212-11215 Godzilla vs. The Smog Monster German lobby cards. Each $5-15.

Left: PO11243 Godzilla vs. The Smog Monster Italian insert. $30-60.

Below: PO12001 Godzilla vs. Gigan Japanese one-sheet. $50-100.

GODZILLA VS. GIGAN

(Earth Defense Order-Godzilla vs. Gigan, released March 12, 1972)

PO#	Title	Country	Format	Price
PO12001	Chikyu Kogeki Meirei-Gojira Tai Gigan	Japanese	1 Sheet	$50-100
PO12002			2 Sheet	75-150
PO12003			2 Sheet (Gigan Powers)	100-200
PO12004			Insert	40-80
PO12005		International	1 Sheet	40-80
PO12006/13			Lobby cards	ea. 15-50
PO12101	Godzilla on Monster Island (1978)	US	1 Sheet	30-50
PO12201	Godzilla vs. Gigan Australia		1 Sheet	25-50
PO12202			Insert	15-30
PO12206	La Planete De Godzilla (1973)	Belgium	1 Sheet	15-30
PO12211	Objectif Terre: Mission Apocalypse (1973)	France	1 Sheet	40-80
PO12212			2 Sheet	50-100
PO12216	Frankenstein's Höllenbrut	Germany	1 Sheet	20-30
PO12217/32			Lobby cards	ea. 5-10
PO12241	Godzilla Contro I Gigante	Italy	1 Sheet	50-100
PO12242			2 Sheet	60-125
PO12243			Insert	30-60
PO12244/51			Lobby cards	ea. 20-40
PO12256	Godzilla Contra Gigan	Mexico	1/2 Sheet	30-50
PO12257/64			Lobby cards	ea. 10-20
PO12271	Godzilla Kontra Gigan	Poland	1 Sheet	50-100
PO12276	Galien, El Monstruo De Las Galaxias, Ataca A La Tierra	Spain	1 Sheet	30-60
PO12281	War of the Monsters	U.K.	1 Sheet	30-60

PO12006-12007 Godzilla vs. Gigan
Japanese lobby cards. Each $15-50.

PO12101 Godzilla vs. Gigan
American one-sheet. $30-50.

PO12202
Godzilla vs.
Gigan
Australian
insert. $15-30.

PO12206
Godzilla vs.
Gigan Belgium
one-sheet.
$15-30.

85

Above: PO12244 Godzilla vs. Gigan Italian lobby card. $20-40.

Left: PO12211 Godzilla vs. Gigan French one-sheet. $40-80.

Above: PO12256 Godzilla vs. Gigan Mexican half-sheet. $30-50.

Right: PO12276 Godzilla vs. Gigan Spanish one-sheet. $30-60.

海底王国のすごいヤツ・メガロ/傷だらけのゴジラ必殺のウルトラC！ 東宝

ゴジラ対メガロ

PO13001 Godzilla vs. Megalon
Japanese one-sheet. $50-100.

GODZILLA VS. MEGALON

(Godzilla vs. Megalon, released March 17, 1973)

PO13001	Gojira Tai Megaro	Japanese	1 Sheet	$50-100
PO13002			2 Sheet (Vertical)	75-150
PO13003			Insert	40-80
PO13004		International	1 Sheet	50-90
PO13005/12			Lobby cards	ea. 15-50
PO13101	Godzilla vs. Megalon (1976)	US	1 Sheet (Style A)	30-60
PO13102			1 Sheet (Style B)	30-60
PO13201	Godzilla vs. Megalon	Australia	Insert	15-30
PO13206	Godzilla 1980 (1976)	Belgium	1 Sheet	15-30
PO13211	Godzilla 1980 (1976)	France	1 Sheet	20-40
PO13212			2 Sheet	30-60
PO13213/20			Lobby cards	ea. 10-20
PO13221	King Kong Dämonen Aus Dem Weltall	Germany	1 Sheet	20-30
PO13222/36			Lobby cards	ea. 5-10
PO13241	Ai Confini Della Realta	Italy	1 Sheet	40-80
PO13242			2 Sheet	50-100
PO13243			Insert	30-60
PO13244/51			Lobby cards	ea. 20-35
PO13261/8	Titanes Planetarios	Mexico	Lobby cards	ea. 10-20
PO13271	Gorgo Y Superman Se Citan En Tokio	Spain	1 Sheet	25-50

PO13005-13008 Godzilla vs. Megalon Japanese lobby cards. Each $15-50.

GIANT AGAINST GIANT... the ultimate battle!

GODZILLA vs MEGALON

DISTRIBUTED BY CINEMA SHARES INTERNATIONAL DISTRIBUTION CORP. IN COLOR

PO13101 Godzilla vs. Megalon American one-sheet. Style A. $30-60.

MONSTER AGAINST MONSTER FOR THE LOST CONTINENT OF MU!

GODZILLA vs. MEGALON

in COLOR·WIDESCREEN

GENERAL AUDIENCES

DISTRIBUTED BY CINEMA SHARES INTERNATIONAL DISTRIBUTION CORP.

PO13102 Godzilla vs. Megalon American one-sheet. Style B. $30-60.

Above: PO13213-13216 Godzilla vs. Megalon French lobby cards. Each $10-20.

Left: PO13201 Godzilla vs. Megalon Australian insert. $15-30

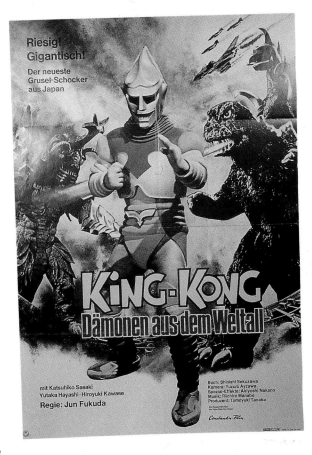

Above: PO13244 Godzilla vs. Megalon Italian lobby card. $20-35.

Left: PO13221 Godzilla vs. Megalon German one-sheet. $20-30.

GODZILLA VS. MECHAGODZILLA
(Godzilla vs. MechaGodzilla, released March 21, 1974)

PO14001	Gojira Tai KaGojira	Japanese	1 Sheet	$50-100
PO14002			2 Sheet (Vertical)	75-150
PO14003			2 Sheet ('Powers Style')	100-200
PO14004			Insert	30-60
PO14005		International	1 Sheet	50-90
PO14006/12			Lobby cards	ea. 15-50
PO14101	Godzilla vs. The Bionic Monster, also released as: Godzilla vs. The Cosmic Monster (1977)	US	1 Sheet (A-Gogos art)	30-60
PO14102			1 Sheet (Style B)	25-50
PO14201	Godzilla Contre Mekanik Monster (1977)	France	1 Sheet	30-60
PO1402			2 Sheet	40-80
PO14206	King Kong Gegen Godzilla	Germany	1 Sheet	20-30
PO14207/18			Lobby cards	ea. 5-10
PO14226	Godzilla Contro I Robot	Italy	1 Sheet	40-80
PO14227			2 Sheet	50-100
PO14228			Insert	30-60
PO14229/36			Lobby cards	ea. 20-40
PO14241/8	Godzilla Contra MechaGodzilla	Mexico	Lobby cards	ea. 10-20
PO14251	Terror MechaGodzilli	Poland	1 Sheet	50-100
PO14256	Godzilla vs. The Bionic Monster, also released as: Godzilla vs. The Cosmic Monster	U.K.	1 Sheet	30-50

PO14001 Godzilla vs. MechaGodzilla
Japanese one-sheet. $50-100.

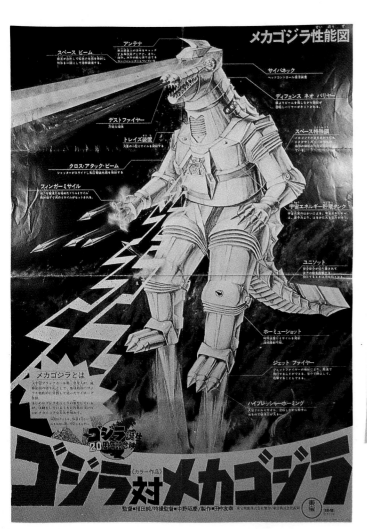

Above: PO14005 Godzilla vs. MechaGodzilla
International one-sheet. $50-90.

Left: PO14003 Godzilla vs. MechaGodzilla
Japanese two-sheet. $100-200.

PO14006-14007 Godzilla vs. MechaGodzilla
Japanese lobby cards. Each $15-50.

PO14101 Godzilla vs. MechaGodzilla
American one-sheet. Style A. $30-60.

PO14102 Godzilla vs. MechaGodzilla
American one-sheet. Style B. $25-50.

PO14226 Godzilla vs. MechaGodzilla
Italian one-sheet. 40-80.

PO14229 Godzilla vs. MechaGodzilla
Italian lobby card. $20-40.

PO14241-14244 Godzilla vs. MechaGodzilla
Mexican lobby cards. Each $10-20.

PO14251 Godzilla vs. MechaGodzilla
Polish poster. $50-100.

TERROR OF MECHAGODZILLA
(MechaGodzilla's Counterattack, released March 15, 1975)

PO15001	MekaGojira No Gyakushu	Japanese	1 Sheet	$60-120
PO15002			2 Sheet (Vertical)	75-150
PO15003			Insert	40-80
PO15004		International	1 Sheet	50-90
PO15005/10			Lobby cards	ea. 15-50
PO15101	Terror of Godzilla (1978)	US	1 Sheet	25-50
PO15201	Les Monstres Su Continent Perdu (1976)	Belgium	1 Sheet	15-30
PO15206	Les Monstres Du Continent Perdu (1976)	France	1 Sheet	40 -80
PO15207			2 Sheet	50-100
PO15211	Die Brut Des Teufels	Germany	1 Sheet	20-30
PO15212/28			Lobby cards	ea. 5-10
PO15236	Distruggete Kong! La Terr E' In Pericolo	Italy	1 Sheet	50-100
PO15237			2 Sheet	60-120
PO15238			Insert	30-60
PO15239/46			Lobby cards	ea. 10-30
PO15251/8	MecaKong	Mexico	Lobby cards	ea. 10-20
PO15266	Powrot MechaGodzilli	Poland	1 Sheet	50-100
PO15271	Monsters From an Unknown Planet	UK	1 Sheet	25-50

PO15001 Terror of MechaGodzilla
Japanese one-sheet. $60-120.

PO15004
Terror of
MechaGodzilla
International
one-sheet.
$50-90.

PO15101 Terror of MechaGodzilla
American one-sheet. $25-50.

PO15005-15006 Terror of MechaGodzilla
Japanese lobby cards. Each $15-50.

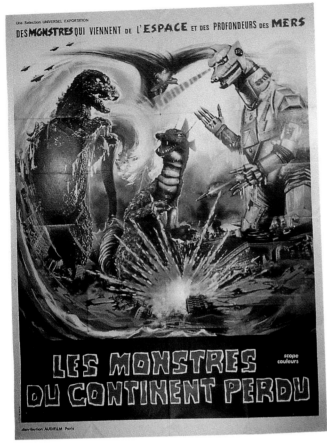

PO15206 Terror of MechaGodzilla
French two-sheet. $50-100.

PO15212-15218 Terror of MechaGodzilla
German lobby cards. $5-10.

PO15266 Terror of MechaGodzilla
Polish one-sheet. $50-100.

PO15271
Terror of
MechaGodzilla
British one-
sheet. $25-50.

GODZILLA 1985

(Godzilla, released December 15, 1984)

PO16001	Gojira	Japanese	1 Sheet	$20-40
PO16002			2 Sheet	60-120
PO16003			2 Sheet (Advance)	100-200
PO16004/11			Lobby cards	ea. 10-20
PO16101	Godzilla 1985 (1985)	US	1 Sheet	10-20
PO16102			Standee	40 -80
PO16201	Godzilla 1985	Australia	Insert	10-20
PO16206	Godzilla Die Rückkehr Des Monster	German	1 Sheet	15-30
PO16207/14			Lobby cards	ea. 5-10
PO16221	De Terugkeer Van Godzilla	Holland	1 Sheet	15-30
PO16226	Godzilla 1985	Mexican	1 Sheet	10-20
PO16231	Godzilla	Spain	1 Sheet	10-20
PO16236	Godzilla, The Legend is Reborn	U.K.	1 Sheet	15-25

Above: PO16001 Godzilla 1985 Japanese one-sheet. $20-40.

Right: PO16002 Godzilla 1985 Japanese two-sheet. $60-120.

PO16101 Godzilla 1985
American one-sheet. $10-20.

PO16003 Godzilla 1985 Japanese
two-sheet. Advance style. $100-200.

PO16207-16208 Godzilla 1985
German lobby cards. Each $5-10.

PO16226 Godzilla 1985
Mexican one-sheet. $10-20.

GODZILLA VS. BIOLLANTE

(Godzilla vs. Biollante, released December 16, 1989)

PO17001	Gojira Tai Biorante	Japanese	1 Sheet	$20-40
PO17002			1 Sheet (Advance)	30-60
PO17003			2 Sheet (Advance)	50-90
PO17004			2 Sheet (Style B)	50-90
PO17005			3 Sheet	100-200
PO17006/13			Lobby cards	ea. 10-20
PO17201	Godzilla Der Urgigant	Germany	1 Sheet	20-40
PO17202/9			Lobby cards	ea. 5-10
PO17221		Thailand	1 Sheet	20-30

PO17001 Godzilla vs. Biollante
Japanese one-sheet. $20-40.

Above:
PO17003
Godzilla vs.
Biollante
Japanese two-
sheet. Advance
style. $50-90.

Right:
PO17006-17008
Godzilla vs.
Biollante
Japanese lobby
cards. Each
$10-20.

PO17221 Godzilla vs. Biollante
Thai one-sheet. $20-30.

PO18001 Godzilla vs. King Ghidora
Japanese one-sheet. $10-20.

PO18002 Godzilla vs. King Ghidora Japanese
one-sheet. Advance style. $25-50.

PO18003 Godzilla vs. King Ghidora Japanese
two-sheet poster. (Advance style). $50-100.

GODZILLA VS. KING GHIDORA

(Godzilla vs. King Ghidora, released December 14, 1991)

PO18001	Gojira Tai Kingu			
	Gidora	Japanese	1 Sheet	$10-20
PO18002			1 Sheet (Advance)	25-50
PO18003			2 Sheet (Advance)	50-100
PO18004			1/2 Sheet Poster	15-25
PO18005/12			Lobby cards	ea.10-20
PO18012			Video 1 Sheet	10-20
PO18201	Godzilla Duell			
	Der Megasaurier	German	1 Sheet	20-40
PO18202/9			Lobby cards	ea. 5-10
PO18216		Thailand	1 Sheet	20-40

Above: PO18005-18008 Godzilla vs. King Ghidora Japanese lobby cards. Each $10-20.

Right: PO201 Godzilla vs. King Ghidora German one-sheet. $20-40.

Above: PO18202-18205 Godzilla vs. King Ghidora German lobby cards. Each $5-10.

Right: PO18216 Godzilla vs. King Ghidora Thai one-sheet. $20-40.

GODZILLA VS. MOTHRA 1992
(Godzilla vs. Mothra, released December 12, 1992)

PO19001	Gojira Tai Mosura	Japanese	1 Sheet	$10-20
PO19002			1 Sheet (Advance)	20-40
PO19003			2 Sheet	30-60
PO19004			2 Sheet (Advance)	40-80
PO19005			3 Sheet	100-100
PO19006/13			Lobby cards	ea. 10-20
PO19201		Thailand	1 Sheet	20-40

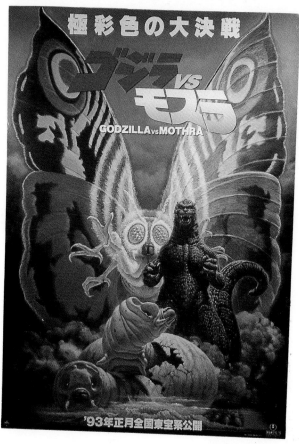

Above: PO19001 Godzilla vs. Mothra Japanese one-sheet. $10-20.

Right: PO19004 Godzilla vs. Mothra Japanese two-sheet. Advance style. $40-80.

PO19006-19009 Godzilla vs. Mothra
Japanese lobby cards. Each $10-20.

PO19010-19013 Godzilla vs. Mothra
Japanese lobby cards. Each $10-20.

GODZILLA VS. MECHAGOZILLA 1993

(Godzilla vs. MechaGodzilla, released December 11, 1993)

PO20001	Gojira Tai Meka-Gojira	Japanese	1 Sheet	$10-20
PO20002			1 Sheet (Advance)	20-40
PO20003			2 Sheet	25-50
PO20004			2 Sheet (Advance)	30-60
PO20005			3 Sheet	100-200
PO20006/13			Lobby cards	ea. 10-20

Above: PO20004 Godzilla vs. MechaGodzilla Japanese two-sheet. Advance style. $30-60.

Left: PO20001 Godzilla vs. MechaGodzilla Japanese one-sheet. $10-20.

PO20006-20009 Godzilla vs. MechaGodzilla Japanese lobby cards. Each $10-20.

PO20010-20013 Godzilla vs. MechaGodzilla Japanese lobby cards. Each $10-20.

PO21001
Godzilla vs.
SpaceGodzilla
Japanese one-
sheet. $10-20.

PO21002 Godzilla vs. SpaceGodzilla
Japanese two-sheet. Advance style. $25-50.

PO21005 Godzilla vs. SpaceGodzilla
Japanese three-sheet. $100-200.

GODZILLA VS. SPACEGODZILLA

(Godzilla vs. SpaceGodzilla, released December 10, 1994)

PO21001	Gojira Tai Supesu			
	Gojira	Japanese	1 Sheet	$10-20
PO21002			1 Sheet (Advance)	15-30
PO21003			2 Sheet	20-40
PO21004			2 Sheet (Advance)	25-50
PO21005			3 Sheet	100-200
PO21006/13			Lobby cards	ea. 10-20

PO21006-21009 Godzilla vs. SpaceGodzilla
lobby cards. Each $10-20.

PO21010-21013 Godzilla vs. SpaceGodzilla
lobby cards. Each $10-20.

GODZILLA VS. DESTROYER
(Godzilla vs. Destroyer, released December 9, 1995)

PO22001	Gojira Tai Desutoroia	Japanese	1 Sheet	$10-20
PO22002			1 Sheet (Advance)	10-20
PO22003			2 Sheet	20-40
PO22004			2 Sheet (Advance)	25-50
PO22005			3 Sheet	100-200
PO22006/13			Lobby cards	ea. 10-20

GODZILLA (1998)

PO23101	Godzilla	US	1 Sheet (Teaser)	$8-15

Posters, Commercial

PO99101	Godzilla vs. Barkley (3 different)	ea. $6-10
PO99002	Godzilla 1984	15-25
PO99002	Godzilla vs. Biollante (2 different)	ea. 10-20
PO99003	Godzilla vs. King Ghidora	15-25
PO99004	Godzilla vs. MechaGodzilla'93	14-20
PO99005	Godzilla vs. SpaceGodzilla	7-12
PO99006	Godzilla vs. Destroyer	8-12
PO99101	Godzilla Paper Collection-Reprint collection of posters and publicity material (Yamakatsu, 1983)	220-260

Above: PO22001 Godzilla vs. Destroyer Japanese one-sheet. $10-20.

Right: PO22004 Godzilla vs. Destroyer Japanese one-sheet. Advance style. $10-20.

PO22006-22009 Godzilla vs. Destroyer Japanese lobby cards. Each $10-20.

PO22010-22013 Godzilla vs. Destroyer Japanese lobby cards. Each $10-20.

PROGRAMS

Japanese

Note: For ease of use, all programs will be listed by their more familiar English titles, rather than their foreign titles.

PP1001	Godzilla	$500-800
PP1101	Godzilla, King of the Monsters	300-600
PP1002	Gigantis, The Fire Monster	400-700
PP1003	King Kong vs. Godzilla	200-300
PP1103	King Kong vs. Godzilla (1970 release)	50 -80
PP1203	King Kong vs. Godzilla (1977 release, style A)	30-50
PP1213	King Kong vs. Godzilla (1977 release, style B)	35-55
PP1004	Godzilla vs. the Thing	150-250
PP1104	Godzilla vs. the Thing (1970 release, style A)	50-90
PP1204	Godzilla vs. the Thing (1970 release, style B)	50-90
PP1005	Ghidrah, the Three Headed Monster	120-225
PP1105	Ghidrah, the Three Headed Monster (1971 release, style A)	50-90
PP1205	Ghidrah, the Three Headed Monster (1971 release, style B)	55-95
PP1006	Monster Zero	100-200
PP1106	Monster Zero (1971 release, style A)	50-90
PP1206	Monster Zero (1971 release, style B)	55-95
PP1007	Godzilla vs. the Sea Monster	100-200
PP1107	Godzilla vs. the Sea Monster (1972 release, style A)	40-80
PP1207	Godzilla vs. the Sea Monster (1972 release, style B)	40-80
PP1008	Son of Godzilla	75-150
PP1108	Son of Godzilla (1973 release, style A)	40-80
PP1208	Son of Godzilla (1973 release, style B)	30-60
PP1009	Destroy all Monsters	175-275
PP1109	Destroy all Monsters (1973 release, style A)	50-90

PP1203 King Kong vs. Godzilla 1977 re-release Japanese program. Style A. $30-50.

Above: PP1104 Godzilla vs. the Thing 1970 re-release Japanese program. Style A. $50-90.

Right: PP1105 Ghidrah, the Three Headed Monster 1971 re-release Japanese program. Style A. $50-90.

PP1006 Monster Zero original
Japanese program. $100-200.

PP1108 Son of Godzilla 1973 re-release
Japanese program. Style A. $40-80.

PP1009 Pop-up centerfold from Destroy All
Monsters original Japanese program. $175-275.

PP1010 Godzilla's Revenge original
Japanese program. $50-100.

PP1111 Godzilla vs. the Smog Monster original
Japanese program. Style B. $50-100.

PP1209	Destroy all Monsters (1973 release, style B)	60-100
PP1010	Godzilla's Revenge	50-100
PP1011	Godzilla vs. the Smog Monster (style A)	50-100
PP1111	Godzilla vs. the Smog Monster (style B)	50-100
PP1012	Godzilla vs. Gigan (style A)	45-90
PP1112	Godzilla vs. Gigan (style B)	40-80
PP1013	Godzilla vs. Megalon (style A)	40-80
PP1113	Godzilla vs. Megalon (style B)	40-80
PP1014	Godzilla vs. MechaGodzilla (style A)	40-80
PP1114	Godzilla vs. MechaGodzilla (style B)	40-80
PP1015	Terror of MechaGodzilla (style A)	45-90
PP1115	Terror of MechaGodzilla (style B)	40-80
PP1401	Godzilla 1983 Festival	20-30
PP1016	Godzilla 1984	10-20
PP1017	Godzilla vs. Biollante	10-20
PP1018	Godzilla vs. King Ghidora	10-20
PP1019	Godzilla vs. Mothra 1992	10-20
PP1020	Godzilla vs. MechaGodzilla 1993	8-15
PP1021	Godzilla vs. SpaceGodzilla	8-15
PP1022	Godzilla vs. Destroyer	8-15

German

PP2001	Godzilla, King of the Monsters	$60-80
PP2002	Gigantis, The Fire Monster	45-60
PP2004	Godzilla vs. The Thing	30-40
PP2006	Monster Zero	30-40
PP2012	Godzilla vs. Gigan	20-30
PP2013	Godzilla vs. Megalon	15-25
PP2014	Godzilla vs. MechaGodzilla (1974)	15-25

PP1401 Godzilla 1983 Festival
Japanese program. $20-30.

PROMOTIONAL ITEMS
Tie-in Merchandise

Chain Store Promotions
PR1001	White Castle Promotion (cups, blow-up, and throwing star) set	$40-50
PR1002	Display for above	50-75

Konica Film
PR2001	Calendar (1994)	$10-15
PR2002	Calendar (1995)	10-15
PR2003	Coin Purse	8-15
PR2004	Tape Measure	8-15
PR2005	Godzilla vs. Mothra Game (1992)	12-20
PR2006	Godzilla vs. SpaceGodzilla Foil Balloon	8-12
PR2007	Godzilla vs. SpaceGodzilla Inflatable	30-50
PR2008	Godzilla vs. SpaceGodzilla 3D Photo	6-10

Theater Items
PR3001	Godzilla Pop-up Book (1954 Theater Giveaway)	$300-500
PR3002	King Kong vs. Godzilla Wonderful Monster Display (1962, Birely's Giveaway)	70-100
PR3003	Godzilla vs. Megalon (U.S.) comic book	20-30
PR3004	Godzilla vs. Megalon (U.S.) pin-back buttons	ea. 15-20
PR4001	Godzilla vs. King Ghidora hologram ticket	30-50
PR4002	Godzilla vs. MechaGodzilla (1993) advance ticket folder	15-25
PR4003	Godzilla vs. SpaceGodzilla advance ticket folder	12-20
PR4004	Godzilla vs. Destroyer advance ticket folder	10-20

Toho Video
PR5001	Godzilla vs. King Ghidora (1992) Ghidora Inflatable	$50-60
PR5002	Godzilla vs. Mothra (1992) Mothra Inflatable	40-50

Press Books/Kits

Not available for sale to the general public, press kits are just as their name implies:

Packs of information about the movies to be used by reviewers, newspapers, etc.. Press books were usually used by theater owners to help in promoting the movie, and usually contain copies of pre-made newspaper ads and photos of the various posters available for use by the theater. Publicity stills are sent out by the releasing company to promote the film and are used mainly for advertising purposes. Most American stills sell very inexpensively, due to the fact that they have been reprinted many times over the years. Original Japanese stills are very difficult to acquire due to the tight control that Toho Studios places on them and early ones can bring very high prices. We have included a few examples below to give you an idea of what press books and kits can sell for.

Press Books
PB1101	Godzilla, King of the Monsters (US, 1956)	$30-50
PB1103	King Kong vs. Godzilla (US, 1963)	20-30
PB1104	Godzilla vs. The Thing (US, 1964)	15-25
PB1109	Destroy All Monsters (US, 1969)	15-25
PB1111	Godzilla vs. The Smog Monster (US, 1972)	10-15

Press Kits
PK2017	Godzilla vs. Biollante	$10-20
PK2020	Godzilla vs. MechaGodzilla	10-20
PK2021	Godzilla vs. SpaceGodzilla	8-15
PK2022	Godzilla vs. Destroyer (Japan, 1995)	8-15

PR1001 White Castle promotional set. $40-50.

Above: PB1104 Godzilla vs. the Thing US press book. $15-25.

Left: PK2020 Godzilla vs. MechaGodzilla Japanese press kit. $10-20.

PR4001 Godzilla vs. King Ghidora hologram ticket. $30-50.

PROPS AND SCRIPTS

Although it is the dream of many a collector to own a prop from one of the Godzilla films, it is almost impossible for the average collector to attempt. What few are known to escape from Toho Studios are usually given to distinguished visitors or put into well-established Japanese collections. If an item is offered to you, please inspect it carefully before you consider buying it. What is the provenance of the item in question? Can it be easily traced back to the studio? Is it offered with any kind of warranty or money-back guarantee? Who is the seller of the item? All these factors must be checked out to both determine whether or not a piece is authentic *and* whether or not you want it.

Most props from the 1950s and early 1960s films have been destroyed or have deteriorated to the point where they are no longer recognizable. In case you are wondering, the earliest surviving head from a Godzilla costume is the one that was used in *Godzilla vs. The Sea Monster*. There are no known full costumes surviving from any film or monster until the 1970s (and even these are barely recognizable). Possibly the most important prop still in existence sits in the Toho Studios office, belonging to Koichi Kawakita. It is the Oxygen Destroyer used in the original 1954 *Godzilla* film.

Collecting scripts is another activity that is gaining considerable popularity. Most scripts that are available today are from the later series (1984-present) of movies, but are still of considerable value to collectors. These items were used by the actors, actresses, producers, and the director of the films. They are of great historical—as well as monetary—value. Many contain information on scenes that would later end up on the cutting room floor. Again, use the same scrutiny that you would use when inspecting a prop to inspect a script. Scripts from the first few films are of the utmost rarity, and are beyond the reach of all but the wealthiest of collectors.

Although we will not attempt to price them, we have included a few pictures of authentic props and scripts for your enjoyment.

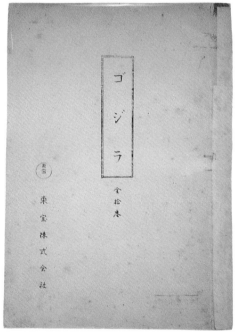

Prop sign from Godzilla vs. MechaGodzilla (G-Force meeting center).

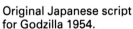

Original Japanese script for Godzilla 1954.

Above: Prop fighter plane from Godzilla 1984.

Left: Prop hats and patch worn by G-Force members in Godzilla vs. MechaGodzilla 1993.

RECORDINGS

Book and Record Sets

RB4612	Giant Monster War (F6-12)	$70-90
RB1001	Destroy All Monsters (1968) (AS-001)	80-100
RB4030	Godzilla's Electric Attack (AM-4030)	60-80
RB4034	Godzilla, Mothra, King Ghidrah-Giant Monster Battle (AM-34)	90-110
RB4040	Godzilla vs. Gigan (AM-40)	90-110
RB4016	Godzilla vs. Hedorah (AM-16)	80-100
RB1099	Godzilla vs. the Sea Monster (1966)	100-130
RB1059	Godzilla's Revenge (1970) (P-59)	60-80
RB1120	Monster Zero (1971) (AS-120)	90-110
RB1110	Mothra vs. Godzilla (1970)	80-100
RB1109	Son of Godzilla (1968)	80-100

RB1001 Destroy All Monsters book and record set. $80-100.
RB1110 Mothra vs. Godzilla book and record set. $80-100.

RL2701 King of the Monsters
Godzilla record. $25-35.

RL2901
Monster Mask
Big March
record. $40-50.

45's

RE1014	Defeat MechaGodzilla/Prayer of Miyarabi (DT-1014)	$20-40
RE1001	Go! Go! Godzilla (DU-1001)	15-30
RE1915	Godzilla (1984) Love Theme (P-1915)	10-20
RE1006	Godzilla & Jet Jaguar-Punch! Punch! Punch! (DT-1006)	20-40
RE1542	Godzilla Forever (K-1542)	20-30
RE1003	Godzilla vs. Hedorah (DC-1003)	30-50
RE1004	Godzilla's Bride/Rock! Rock! Godzilla (DS-1004)	30-50
RE1003	Godzilla March/Destroy Gigan (DU-1003)	30-50
RE1027	Monster Christmas/Monster Game (AS-1027)	20-40
RE4536	Rock on Godzilla (SCS-536)	30-50
RE4441	Song of Mothra (TV41)	15-25
RE2001	We are the Monster Force (DC-1001)	20-35

LP's

RL1001	Akira Ifukube-SFX Film Music Best Collection Vol.1-4 (TP-72410-3)	ea. $10-15
RL1101	An Evening of Special Effects Film Music (K20G-7169/70)	20-30
RL1201	Deluxe Edition Godzilla (picture disc) (K25G-7236)	25-40
RL1401/10	Film Works of Akira Ifukube, The Vol. 1-10 (K22G-7043/52)	ea. 10-15
RL1501	Godzilla (AX-8100) & (K22G-7222)	30-40
RL1502	Godzilla 2 (AX-8112) & (K22G-7239)	20-30
RL1503	Godzilla 3 (AX-8147) & (K22G-7247)	20-30
RL1601	Godzilla (Drama) (K18G-7191/2)	10-15
RL1701	Godzilla (1984, w/BGM) (K28G-7226)	15-20
RL1901	Godzilla King of the Monsters (10 volume cassette set) (JTN-1471/80)	80-120
RL9312	Godzilla, King of the Monsters (WLP-312)	10-20
RL2001	Godzilla-Original BGM Collection 1 (CX-7020)	25-40
RL2002	Godzilla-Original BGM Collection 2 (CX-7021)	25-40
RL2101	Godzilla Legend (K28G-7110)	12-20
RL2102	Godzilla Legend II (K28G-7171)	12-20
RL2103	Godzilla Legend III (K28G-7225)	12-20
RL2301	Godzilla Theme Song Collection (JBX-2039)	20-30
RL2401	History of Godzilla Vol.1 (AS20-11)	12-20
RL2402	History of Godzilla Vol.2 (AS20-12)	12-20
RL2403	History of Godzilla Vol.3 (AS20-13)	12-20
RL2501	It's the Mask, It's the Monster, All Marching! (DX-1001)	25-35
RL2601	King Kong vs. Godzilla (drama w/BGM) (K18G-7158/9)	15-20
RL2701	King of the Monsters Godzilla (DX-1004)	25-35
RL2801	Let's Sing! Let's Dance! TV Theme Songs (DX-1009)	20-30
RL2901	Monster Mask Big March (DR-1001)	40-50
RL3001	Monster Zero (Drama) (K18G-7123/4)	12-20
RL3101	Ostinato (K28G-7318)	12-20
RL3201/10	SF Special Effects Movie Music Vol. 1-10 (K22G-7111-20)	ea. 12-20
RL3214	SF Special Effects Movie Music-Special Record (17DH-5806-01)	15-25
RL3215	SF Special Effects Fair-Special Recording (17DH-5812-03)	15-25
RL3301	Sound Effect of Godzilla 1 (T23-1073)	12-20
RL3302	Sound Effect of Godzilla 2 (T23-1074)	12-20
RL3401	Super Monster Godzilla Film Series #1 (CS-7190)	15-25
RL3402	Super Monster Godzilla Film Series #2 (CZ-7057)	15-25
RL3403	Super Monster Godzilla Film Series #3 (CZ-7058)	15-25
RL3404	Super Monster Godzilla Film Series #4 (CZ-7068)	15-25
RL3405	Super Monster Godzilla Film Series #5 (CZ-7069)	15-25
RL3501	Toho SPFX Film Collection #1 (AS20-1)	10-15
RL3502	Toho SPFX Film Collection #2 (AS20-7)	10-15
RL3601	Toho SPFX Film Pops Graffiti (K23G-7273)	10-15

RE1542 Godzilla Forever record. $20-30.
RE1915 Godzilla Love theme record. $10-20.

RL1901 Godzilla King of the Monsters 10 cassette box set. $80-120.

RL9312 Godzilla, King of the Monsters record. $10-20.

RL3601 Toho SPFX Film Pops Graffiti record. $10-15.

109

CD's

CD5345	Godzilla 1954 (TYCY-5345)	$18-28
CD5346	Godzilla Raids Again (TYCY-5346)	18-28
CD5347	King Kong vs. Godzilla (TYCY-5347)	18-28
CD5348	Godzilla vs. the Thing (TYCY-5348)	18-28
CD5349	Ghidrah, the Three Headed Monster (TYCY-5349)	18-28
CD5350	Monster Zero (TYCY-5350)	18-28
CD5351	Godzilla vs. the Sea Monster (TYCY-5351)	18-28
CD5352	Son of Godzilla (TYCY-5352)	18-28
CD5353	Destroy All Monsters (TYCY-5353)	18-28
CD5354	Godzilla's Revenge (TYCY-5354)	18-28
CD5355	Godzilla vs. the Smog Monster (TYCY-5355)	18-28
CD5356	Godzilla vs. Gigan (TYCY-5356)	18-28
CD5357	Godzilla vs. Megalon (TYCY-5357)	18-28
CD5358	Godzilla vs. MechaGodzilla (TYCY-5358)	18-28
CD5359	Terror of MechaGodzilla (TYCY-5359)	18-28
CD5360	Godzilla 1984 (TYCY-5360)	18-28
CD7021	Godzilla 1984 (230A-7022)	20-30
CD5361	Godzilla vs. Biollante (TYCY-5361)	18-28
CD5122	Godzilla vs. Biollante (TYCY-5122)	20-30
CD5362	Godzilla vs. King Ghidora (TYCY-5362)	18-28
CD5269	Godzilla vs. Mothra'92 (TYCY-5269)	26-38
CD5363	Godzilla vs. Mothra '92 (TYCY-5363)	20-30
CD5364	Godzilla vs. MechaGodzilla '93 (TYCY-5364)	28-38
CD1291	Godzilla vs. SpaceGodzilla (KTCR-1291)	28-38
CD1031	Godzilla vs. SpaceGodzilla (KTCR-1031/2)	38-60
CD5468	Godzilla vs. Destroyer (TYCY-5468)	23-33
CD2001	Akira Ifukube Tribute Concert (LD32-5077)	28-38
CD2001	An Evening of Special Effects Film Music (K32X-7034)	28-38
CD2003	Artistry of Akira Ifukube Vol.4 (KICC-178)	28-38
CD5464	Best Selected Music From Godzilla- Then (TYCY-5464)	18-28
CD5465	Best Selected Music From Godzilla- Now (TYCY-5465)	18-28
CD2101	Complete Recordings-Akira Ifukube (TYCY-5215/6)	35-55
CD2109	Complete Recordings-Akira Ifukube-Toho SFX Film Music #9 (TYCY-5342/3)	44-60
CD2110	Complete Recordings-Akira Ifukube-Toho SFX Film Music #10 (TYCY-5267/8)	44-60
CD2111	Complete Recordings-Akira Ifukube-Toho SFX Film Music #11 (TYCY-5469/70)	40-55
CD2301	Contatto Con L'Oriente (SLCD-1001)	26-38
CD2004	Film Music of Masaru Sato #4 (SLCS-7104)	20-30
CD2201/10	Film Works of Akira Ifukube, The #1-10 (SLCS-5050/9) ea.	20-30
CD2300	Godzilla (230A-7021)	20-30
CD2005	Godzilla (KICA-2211)	18-28
CD2006	Godzilla Legend (KICA-72/3/4)	50-75
CD7032	Godzilla Legend-Chronology 1 (K32X-7032)	28-40
CD7033	Godzilla Legend-Chronology 2 (K32X-7033)	28-40
CD5078	Godzilla & Monster Movie Music Collection #1 (VICL-5078)	20-30
CD5079	Godzilla & Monster Movie Music Collection #2 (VICL-5079)	20-30
CD2007	Godzilla's Sorrow (SRCL-3750)	15-25
CD2008	Godzilla Symphonic Fantasia (VPCD-81036/7)	35-50
CD2009	Godzilla Vocal Collection (VICL-5083)	20-30
CD2010	Godzilla vs. King Ghidora (BCCE-9001)	40-55
CD5096	History of Godzilla Vol.1 (APCF-5096)	18-28

CD5097	History of Godzilla Vol.2 (APCF-5097)	18-28
CD2531	Howl (SRCL-2531)	15-25
CD2011	King of the Monsters (KICA-2201/10)	250-350
CD2012	Legend of Godzilla (CDS-15)	20-30
CD2013	Ostinato (K32X-7037) & (KICA-2212)	28-40
CD2301/10	SF Special Effects Movie Music #1-10 (KICA-2031/40) ea.	16-26
CD2940	Song of Mothra (TODT-2940)	8-16
CD2014	Sound Effects of Godzilla (TOCT-8789/90)	32-45
CD2015	Symphonic Concert-Godzilla (SLCS-5029)	26-40
CD2016	Symphonic Fantasia (bonus CD) (YMCC-0001)	40-50
CD2017	Symphonic Ode-Gotama The Buddah (LD32-5105)	26-40
CD5412	Toho Monster Movie March Music (TYCY-5412)	20-30
CD5344	Toho Monster Movie March Music #2 (TYCY-5344)	18-28
CD5412	Toho SPFX Film March Music (TYCY-5412)	22-32
CD2401/8	Toho SFX Film Music #1-8 (LD25-5033/48) & (TYCY-5195/206) ea.	45-65
CD2018	Tribute to Godzilla (VICL-8030)	15-25
CD2019	World of Akira Ifukube (TYCY-5217/8)	45-65

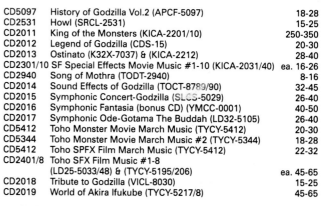

CD5352 and 5357 Son of Godzilla and Godzilla vs. Megalon soundtrack CD's. Each $18-28.

CD2010 Godzilla vs. King Ghidora CD. $40-55. CD5465 Best Selected Music From Godzilla-Now CD. $18-28.

CD2201-2210 King of the Monsters compact disc box set. $250-350.

CD5412 and CD 5344 Toho Monster Movie March Music Volume 1 and 2 compact discs. Each $18-30.

SCHOOL & OFFICE SUPPLIES

Art Pads
SC1001	Godzilla vs. Gigan	$20-30
SC1002	Godzilla Monsters	20-30

Note Pads
SC2001	Godzilla vs. Biollante	$8-15
SC2002	Godzilla vs. King Ghidora	8-15
SC2003	Godzilla vs. Mothra	5-10
SC2004	Godzilla vs. MechaGodzilla	4-8
SC2005	Godzilla vs. SpaceGodzilla	4-7
SC2006	Godzilla vs. Destroyer	3-6

Pencils/Pens
SC3001	Godzilla vs. King Ghidora pen	$5-8
SC3002	Godzilla vs. Mothra pen	5-8
SC3003	Godzilla vs. MechaGodzilla pen	5-8
SC3004	Godzilla Flower Monster pen	5-8
SC3005	LitGodzi Series Pens (Godzilla, Little Godzilla, Mothra, Rodan, and SpaceGodzilla)	ea. 4-7
SC3101	Godzilla vs. Mothra pencil	3-6
SC3102	Godzilla vs. MechaGodzilla pencil	3-6
SC3103	Godzilla vs. SpaceGodzilla pencil	3-6
SC3104	Godzilla vs. Destroyer pencil	3-6
SC3105	Toho Diorama Pencil Set	10-15

Pencil Boxes
SC3101	Godzilla, King of the Monsters	$10-20
SC3102	Godzilla vs. Biollante	8-15
SC3103	Godzilla vs. Mothra Pencil Can (1992)	8-10

Stamp Sets
Amada
SC4001	Godzilla Surecut (stamp dispenser, 1992)	$10-18

Bandai
SC4001	SD Godzilla Stamp Monster 7 (1994)(1 1/2" plastic figures w/ stamps: Godzilla, G-Force Mogera, SpaceGodzilla, King Ghidora, Mothra adult, MechaGodzilla 1993, and Baby Godzilla)	set $15-25

Sticker Sets
SC5001	Brilliant Godzilla Series (3 different packs, Amada 1992)	ea.$ 3-5
SC5002	Godzilla Action Stickers (4 different packs, Imperial, 1985)	ea. 6-10
SC5003	Godzilla Cartoon Stickers (HBP, 1979)	8-12

SC1001-1002 Two different Godzilla art pads. Each $20-30.

SC4001 Super deformed Godzilla stamp set. MIB $15-25.

TOYS

TC1001 Big Scale Godzilla series toys. SpaceGodzilla and King Ghidora pictured. Each $7-12.

TC1008 Godzilla FB collection series three. Mothra, MechaKing Ghidora and Battra pictured. Each $1-2.

Candy Toys
Bandai

TC1001   **Big Scale Godzilla Series (1993-94)**
Godzilla, G-Force Mogera, King Ghidora, Little Godzilla, MechaKing Ghidora, MechaGodzilla'93, and SpaceGodzillaea. $7-12
Series Continues as Super Godzilla (1995)

Glowing Godzilla Series (1993)
Godzilla, Baby Godzilla, Battra (adult & larva), Biollante, Fire Rodan, Gigan, Garuda, King Ghidora, MechaKing Ghidora, MechaGodzilla'74, MechaGodzilla'93, Minya, Mothra (adult), and Super MechaGodzilla   ea. 3-6

TC1003   **Godzilla Big Assortment (w/card, 1991)**
Angilas, Gigan, Gorosaurus, Hedorah, King Ghidora, MechaGodzilla, Minya, Mothra (adult)   ea. 4-6

TC1004   **Godzilla Big Assortment (w/stamp, 1992)**
Godzilla, Gezora, Kamakiras, King Seesar, Kumonga, Mogera, Mothra (larva's w/egg), Sanda, Titanosaurus, and Varan   ea. 4-6

TC1005   **Godzilla Company Series 1 & 2**
(SD 1" Plastic Figures, 1994, 95)
Godzilla 1954, 55, 62, 64, 68, 73, 84, 91, 93, Burning Godzilla, Angilas, Baby Godzilla, Battra (adult & larva), Biollante, Ebirah, Fire Rodan, Ghidrah, Gorosaurus, King Ghidora, King Seesar, MechaKing Ghidora, MechaGodzilla'93, Minya, Mogera, Mothra (adult & larva), SpaceGodzilla, Super MechaGodzilla, Super X, Super X-2, and Titanosaurus   ea. 2-3

Godzilla FB Collection (Super Deformed)

TC1006   Series 1 (1993)
Godzilla'93, Super MechaGodzilla'93, Rodan'93, Baby Godzilla, Megalon, Hedorah, Minya, Kumonga, Kamakiras, Baragon, Varan, Gabara, Ebirah, Gorosaurus & Angilas   ea. $1-2

TC1007   Series 2 (1994)
Godzilla'94, Little Godzilla, Mogera, SpaceGodzilla, Gigan, Mothra (larva), MechaGodzilla, King Ghidora   ea. 1-2

TC1008   Series 3 (1995)
Godzilla'95, Destroyer (final form), Biollante, MechaKing Ghidora, Mothra (adult), Battra (adult & larva), and Rodan ea. 1-2

TC1009   **Godzilla is Go Series (1994)**
Godzilla, SpaceGodzilla, MechaGodzilla'93, &
G-Force Mogera   ea. 6-10
Godzilla 1995 and Destroyer (final form)   ea. 7-12
TC1010   **Godzilla Legend (2" plastic kits, 1992)**
Godzilla, Mothra (adult), SD Godzilla & Minya,
SD MechaGodzilla   ea. 6-12
TC1011   **Godzilla Legend (2" plastic kits, 1992)**
King Ghidora & Tokyo Tower, Mothra (adult & larva),
Godzilla & Osaka Castle, Rodan & Mothra Larva   ea. 7-13
TC1012   **Godzilla Legend (3" plastic kits, 1992)**
Godzilla, SD Godzilla & Minya, SD MechaGodzilla, and Mothra ea. 7-13

Godzilla Proclamation Series (Two 1 1/2" Figures per box, 20 total) TC1013
Series 1 (1993)
Godzilla'93 & MechaGodzilla, Godzilla '91 & MechaKing
Ghidora, Godzilla & Rodan, Godzilla & Angilas,
Godzilla'64 & Mothra, Godzilla'66 & Ebirah, Little Godzilla
& SpaceGodzilla, Mogera & G-Force Mogera, Mothra'92
and Battra, Varan & Magma   ea. $1-2
TC1014   Series 2 (1995)
Godzilla'95 & Destroyer (final form), Godzilla Jr. &
Destroyer (crab form), Gigan & Megalon, MechaGodzilla &
Titanosaurus, Hedorah & Biollante, Baragon & Gorosaurus,
King Ghidrah & Rodan, Godzilla'67 & Kamakiras,
Godzilla'93 & Rodan'93, Battra (larva) & Godzilla'62 ea. 1-2

Godzilla Sofubi Series (Soft Vinyl)
TC1015   Series 1 (1992)
Godzilla, Gigan, Battra (larva), Mothra (larva), King Ghidora,
and MechaGodzilla   ea. $4-8
TC1016   Series 2 (1993)
Godzilla'93, Baby Godzilla, Fire Rodan, King Ghidora,
MechaGodzilla'93, and Super MechaGodzilla'93   ea. 4-8
TC1017   **Godzilla Tanjo (Birth) 1995 (1" figures in egg)**
Godzilla, Mogera, SpaceGodzilla, Angilas, Little Godzilla,
Baragon, Gorosaurus, Mothra (larva), King Ghidora,
and MechaKing Ghidora   ea. 2-5

TC1018   **Go Go Godzilla Series (1993)**
Godzilla, Mothra (adult), Battra (larva), King Ghidrah, Biollantea. 6-10
TC1019   **Heat Up Godzilla (1995) (two per capsule)**
Godzilla'95, Destroyer (final stage), Destroyer (flying),
SpaceGodzilla, G-Force Mogera, Little Godzilla, Biollante,
Super MechaGodzilla, Rodan'93, King Ghidora, Battra
(adult & larva), MechaKing Ghidora, Mothra (adult & larva) ea. 1-2
High Grade Godzilla Series
TC1020   Series 1 (1994)
Godzilla'94, King Ghidora, SuperMechaGodzilla, G-Force
Mogera, Little Godzilla, and SpaceGodzilla   ea. $5-8
TC1021   Series 2 (1995)
Godzilla'95, Destroyer (final form), Mothra (adult),
Battra (adult), MechaKing Ghidora, and Biollante ea. 5-8
TC1022   **Hyper Real Godzilla Series (1995)**
Godzilla & Super X-ll, Destroyer (final form) & Jet Fighter,
G-Force Mogera & Maser Tank, MechaGodzilla 1993 &
Garuda, SpaceGodzilla & Land Mogera w/Star Falcon ea. 5-8
TC1023   **Real Action Godzilla (Theater Giveaway, 1993)**
Godzilla, Fire Rodan, and MechaGodzilla 1993   ea. 6-10
Real Godzilla, Boxed Series (1992)
TC1024   Part 1 (1992)
Godzilla w/base $8-14
TC1025   Part 2 (2" Plastic Figure w/base, 1993)
Godzilla 1964, Godzilla, 1991, Godzilla 1993, Biollante,
MechaKing Ghidora, MechaGodzilla, and Rodan   ea. 5-10
TC1026   Part 3 (2" Plastic Figure & vehicle, 1993)
Godzilla, Biollante, Ghidrah, MechaKing Ghidora,
MechaGodzilla 2, and Rodan, with vehicles: A Cycle Light
Ray, Atomic Heat Ray Cannon, KIDS, Maser Cannon and
Trailer, Maser Jet, Maser Tank 90 & 92, Super X-2, and SY-3ea. 4-8
TC1027   Part 4 (One each Plastic & Rubber per box, 1993)
Godzilla'84 & Shockiras, MechaKing Ghidora & Dorat,
Biollante & Rose Biollante, Mothra (adult) & Cosmos,
Battra (larva) & Godzillasaurus   ea. 5-9

TC1009 Godzilla is Go series
(MechaGodzilla'93). MIB $6-10.

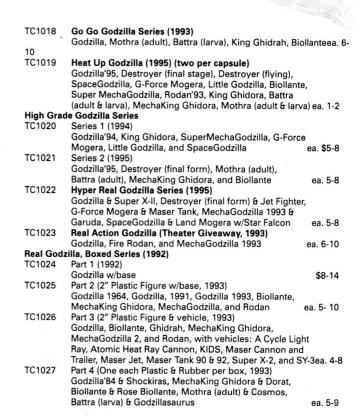

TC1015 Godzilla Sofubi series one. Gigan, Battra, MechaKing
Ghidora, MechaGodzilla and Godzilla. Each $4-8.

TC1017 Godzilla Tanjo small figures.
MechaKing Ghidora, SpaceGodzilla, Little
Godzilla and Mothra pictured. Each $2-5.

TC1018 Go Go Godzilla series. Mothra
and Godzilla pictured. Each MIB $6-10.

Real Godzilla, Capsule Series

TC1028   Part 1 (2" painted plastic figures, 1992)
Godzilla 1991, MechaKing Ghidora, MechaGodzilla, and
Mothra (adult and larva's)   ea. $6-10

TC1029   Part 2 (2" painted plastic figures, 1992)
Godzilla 1992, Battra (adult & larva), Gigan, & King Ghidorea. 6-10

TC1030   Part 3 (2" painted plastic figures, 1992)
Godzilla, Biollante, King Ghidora, MechaKing Ghidora,
MechaGodzilla, and Rodan   ea. 7-11

TC1031   Part 4 (Plastic Ball & Socket Figures, 1993)
Godzilla, Fire Rodan, Little Godzilla, & MechaGodzilla (original)ea. 4-8

TC1032   **SD Godzilla Part 1** (2" Painted figures, 1992)
Godzilla, Gigan, MechaKing Ghidora, MechaGodzilla,
and Mothra (larva)   ea. 4-8

Sunshine Godzilla Series

TC1033   Series 1 (1994)
Rodan, King Seesar, Angilas, MechaGodzilla, & Mothra (larva)ea. $3-6

TC1034   Series 2 (1995) (two per capsule)
Godzilla'95 'A', Godzilla'95 'B', Destroyer (final form),
Destroyer (crab form), Destroyer (flying), SpaceGodzilla
(normal & flying), & Minya   ea. 1-2

TC1035   **Super Godzilla Series (1995)**
Godzilla 1954   20-25
Godzilla'95   7-11
Destroyer (final form)   7-11
Godzilla Jr.   8-12

TC1036   **Super Real Godzilla Series**
(3' painted plastic figures, 1992)
Godzilla, Angilas, Baragon, Gigan, King Ghidora,
MechaGodzilla, & Rodan   ea. 8-12

TC1037   **Super Real Godzilla Series**
(1994)
Godzilla & MechaKing Ghidora, Godzilla & Super
MechaGodzilla, Godzilla & SpaceGodzilla, & Godzilla,
Little Godzilla & G-Force Mogera   ea. 6-10

Morinaga

TC1038   **Godzilla Chocolate (1994,1995)**
(two per box)
MechaKing Ghidora, Hedora, Biollante, Kamakiras,
Gorosaurus, Maser Tank, Baragon, Varan, Cosmo Clock,
Godzilla, Mothra larva, Titanosaurus, Maser Cannon,
Moonlight SY-3, Rodan, MechaGodzilla 1993, Jet Jaguar,
Kumonga, Super MechaGodzilla, Garuda, Fire Rodan,
Tokyo Tower, Minya, Mothra w/egg, Ebirah, MechaGodzilla
1974, Gigan, X-UFO, KIDS, Kilaak-UFO, Super X, Super XII,
Battra Adult, Battra Larva, Baby Godzilla, Submarine,
Black Hole-UFO, Diet Building, Angilas, King Seesar,
Manda, Little Godzilla, Mothra adult, and SpaceGodzilla   ea. $1-2

TC1039   **Godzilla World (1994)**
(all w/Vacu-form base) Godzilla (1994), Mothra (larva),
King Ghidora, Mogera, Fire Rodan, MechaGodzilla (1993),
SpaceGodzilla, Little Godzilla, Battra (adult), & Godzilla (1954)ea. 1-2

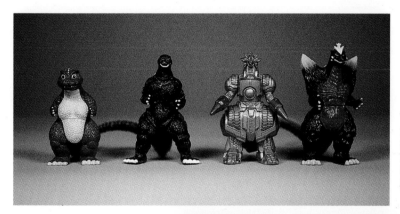

TC1020 High Grade Godzilla series one. Little Godzilla, Godzilla, G-Force Mogera, and SpaceGodzilla pictured. Each $5-8.

TC1021 High Grade Godzilla series two. MechaKing Ghidora, Biollante, Godzilla and Destroyer pictured. Each $5-8.

Left: TC1027 Real Godzilla boxed series. Biollante with Rose Biollante from series four pictured. Each $5-9.

Above: TC1038 Morinaga Godzilla Chocolate toy monsters. Complete set pictured. Each $1-2.

DIE CAST TOYS

Bullmark		Loose	MIB
DC1001	Angilas	$300-500	$700-1000
DC1002	Baragon (green)	75-100	125-175
DC1003	Baragon (blue)	80-120	150-200
DC1004	Gigan	150-200	250-350
DC1005	Godzilla (green)	40-60	100-150
DC1006	Godzilla (brown)	60-80	125-175
DC1007	King Ghidrah	125-175	225-325
DC1008	King Ghidrah (Black Highlights)	125-175	225-325
DC1009	MechaGodzilla	100-125	200-250
DC1010	Mogera	never released	
DC1011	Mothra	never released	
Popy			
DC1012	MechaGodzilla II	$150-200	$300-400

DC1001 Bullmark Die-cast Angilas
(front and back). MIB $700-1000.

DC1002-1003 Bullmark die-cast Baragon (green and blue).
Loose prices: $75-100 (green), $80-120 (blue).

DC1007 and DC1004 Bullmark die-cast King Ghidrah and Gigan.
Loose prices: $125-175 (King Ghidrah), $150-200 (Gigan).

DC1005 and DC1006 Bullmark die-cast Godzilla (green and brown). Loose prices, $40-60 (green), $60-80 (brown).

DC1009 and DC1012 Bullmark die-cast MechaGodzilla and Popy die-cast MechaGodzilla. Loose prices: $125-175 (Bullmark), $150-200 (Popy).

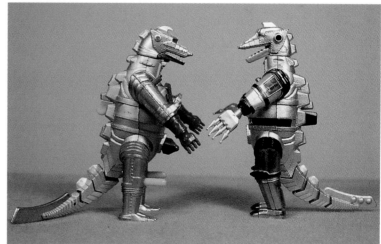

Side views of the two MechaGodzilla's. Bullmark version on the left, Popy on the right.

Boxes for the Bullmark die-cast series.

Above: ET1004 Godzilla and MechaGodzilla box set figures. $150-200.

Right: Box for ET1004, Godzilla and MechaGodzilla box set.

ET1005 Transforming Mogera. MIB price $100-150.

ELECTRONIC TOYS

Bandai

(DX Series-Battery Operated)		
ET1001	Godzilla 1993 (1993)	$50-80
ET1002	Heat Walking Godzilla (1995)	80-110
ET1003	MechaGodzilla 1993 (1993)	80-110
ET1004	Godzilla & MechaGodzilla Box set (1993)	150-200
ET1005	Transforming Mogera (1994)	100-150
ET1006	Powerful Walk Godzilla (1994)	75-100
ET1007	Spark Walk SpaceGodzilla (1994)	80-110
ET1008	Super Walk Destroyer (1995)	80-100
(Real Action Series-Battery Operated)		
ET1009	Destroyer (1995)	55-75
ET1010	Godzilla 1954 style (1994)	60-80
ET1011	Godzilla 1989 style (1993)	55-75
ET1012	Godzilla 1995 style (1995)	55-75
ET1013	King Ghidora (1994)	70-90
ET1014	SpaceGodzilla (1994)	55-75
(Real Hobby Series-Battery Operated)		
ET1015	#5 Godzilla 1964 (1983)	200-300
	(Remote Control)	
ET1016	King Scale Godzilla (1993)	220-280
	(Control is Masér Tank)	
ET1017	King Scale MechaGodzilla 1993 (1993)	220-280
	(Control is Masér Tank)	
ET1018	Radioactive Attack Godzilla (1995)	170-240
	(Control is Super X-III)	

Characon

(Remote Controlled)		
ET2001	Godzilla (1983)	$60-90
ET2002	MechaGodzilla (1983)	80-120

Marui

(Remote Controlled)		
ET3001	Godzilla 1954 style	$550-750
ET3002	Godzilla 1989 style	550-750
ET3003	Mothra (larva)	350-500
ET3004	King Ghidrah (not yet released)	

Popy

(Mecha-Series-Remote Controlled)		
ET4001	Godzilla (1978)	$125-175
ET4002	MechaGodzilla (1978)	125-175

Sega

ET5001	Go Go Riding Godzilla (1995)	$60-120

Yutaka

ET6001	Remocon Godzilla (1992-1995)	$20-30
	(different box for each year)	

Above: ET1008 Super Walk Destroyer. MIB $80-100.

Right: ET1012 and ET1009 Real Action Godzilla (1995) and Destroyer. MIB prices $55-75 each.

ET1014, ET1010 and ET1011. Real Action SpaceGodzilla, Godzilla (1954) and Godzilla (1989). MIB prices $60-80 (Godzilla 1954), $55-75 each for the other two.

REAL HOBBY SERIES no.5

TOHO SCOPE
東宝株式会社

大怪獣ゴジラ

現われる！

★モスラ対ゴジラの"ゴジラ"を極限のディテールで完全再現！
★口の中、眼球、背びれが発光装置セットで点滅する！
★スクリーンの重量感たっぷりの 全長60cm 全高30cm の超ビッグモデル！
（発光装置、単3乾電池付）
●パッケージの写真（イラスト）と製品とは、多少異なりますのでご了承ください。
●本商品は組立キットです。（対象年令は10歳以上）

ET1015 Real Hobby Series Godzilla
with light-up fins. MIB $200-300.

Above: ET1017 King Scale
MechaGodzilla. MIB price
$220-280.

Left: ET1016 King Scale
Godzilla with Maser tank
controller. MIB $220-280.

ET1018 Radioactive Attack Godzilla with light-up
fins and Super X-III controller. MIB $170-240.

ET2001 Characon remote controlled
Godzilla. MIB $60-90.

ET2002 Characon remote controlled
MechaGodzilla. MIB $80-120.

ET6001 Yutaka Remocon Godzilla
still in box. MIB $20-30.

FIGURES & PLAY SETS
Bandai

FT1001   Careful World Godzilla (1993)
(3" figure box set) Godzilla, Gigan, Battra (adult), Battra
(larva), King Ghidora, MechaKing Ghidora, Mecha
Godzilla, Mothra (larva), and Mothra (adult)   set $75-100

FT1002   Charanporan (irresponsible) Series (1987)
(Godzilla, Ghidrah, and Rodan)   ea. 15-25

FT1003   DX Real Godzilla Box Set (3" Figures, 1993)
(Godzilla, MechaGodzilla 1993, and Fire Rodan
w/Makuhari Base)   set 18-25

FT1004   Godzilla Battle Special Set A w/G-Force Dock
(Godzilla 1962, Super MechaGodzilla'93, Battra (adult),
Mothra (adult & larva), MechaKing Ghidora, Gigan, Rodan,
Godzilla 1994, SpaceGodzilla, Titanosaurus, &
MechaGodzilla 2)   set 18-30

FT1005   Godzilla Battle Special Set B w/Chiba
Stadium & Fukuoka Tower (Godzilla 1964, King Ghidora,
Fire Rodan, Angilas, King Seesar, MechaGodzilla 1993,
Megalon, MechaGodzilla 1974, Mogera, SpaceGodzilla,
Godzilla 1993, Baragon, and Battra (larva))   set 18-30

FT1006   Godzilla Eight Giant Monsters Line-up (1992)
(Godzilla, Gigan, King Seesar, King Ghidora, Mothra
(larva & adult), Rodan, and MechaGodzilla)   set 60-85

FT1007   Godzilla Felt Set (1984)
(3" felt figures) Godzilla, Baragon, Ghidrah, Minya,
Mothra, and Rodan   ea. 15-25
6" large felt Godzilla   20-30

FT1009   Godzilla Battle Arena 'A' (1995)
(Godzilla'95, Destroyer (final form), Godzilla'94,
Baby Godzilla, G-Force Mogera, Angilas, Megalon,
MechaGodzilla'93, Ebirah, Gorosaurus, King Ghidora,
Mothra (adult) & Garuda)   set 12-20

FT1010   Godzilla Battle Arena 'B' (1995)
(Godzilla, MechaGodzilla, SpaceGodzilla, Little Godzilla,
King Seesar, Mothra (larva), Hedorah, Baragon, Gigan,
Destroyer (flying), Battra (adult), Rodan'93, &
MechaKing Ghidora)   set 12-20

FT1011   Godzilla Super 3-D Battle set
(Godzilla, G-Force Mogera, King Ghidora, Little Godzilla,

FT1002 Charanporan Series: King Ghidrah,
Godzilla, and Rodan. MIB each $15-25.

FT1006 Godzilla Eight Giant Monsters
Line-up boxed set. MIB $60-85.

FT1011 Godzilla Super 3-D
Battle set. MIB $40-55.

FT1014 Kaiju Series
rubber Godzilla with
box. MIB $75-110.

FT1015 SD Godzilla Giant Monsters
finger puppet set. MIB $15-25.

FT1015 Three Giant Monsters
Big Battle Set. MIB $50-80.

FT2001 Cyborg
MechaGodzilla
figure. Fires
missiles from
hands and chest.
Loose $350-500.

FT2002 Missile Firing MechaGodzilla.
Smaller than FT2001 figure, fires
missiles from chest. Loose $200-400.

	MechaGodzilla & SpaceGodzilla)	set 40-55
FT1012	Godzilla Super Battle Line-up	
	(Godzilla, Destroyer, Space Godzilla, MechaGodzilla '93,	
	and King Ghidora)	set 35-50
FT1013	Godzilla & MechaGodzilla two pack	set 10-15
FT1014	Kaiju Series Godzilla (1983)	75-110
FT1015	SD Godzilla Giant Monster Set (1992)	
	(10 -1" finger puppets in box set)	set 15-25
FT1016	Three Giant Monsters Big Battle Set (1992)	
	(Godzilla, Battra (larva), Mothra (larva), and building)	set 50-80
FT1017	Toko Toko Godzilla vs. Mothra	8-12

Bullmark

FT2001	Cyborg MechaGodzilla (missile firing, 1975)	$350-500
FT2002	MechaGodzilla, missile firing -small (1974)	200-400
FT2003	Mini Mini Monster Set (1975)	
	(18 figure, 2" rubber monster set, includes Godzilla, Mothra	
	(adult), Mogera, King Ghidrah, Rodan, Angilas, Mecha	
	Godzilla, Gigan, Baragon, Gabara, & other monsters)set	100-150
FT2004	Sparking Godzilla (1972)	400-600

FT2004 Bullmark Sparking Godzilla. $400-600.

FT3001 Godzilla Monster Army box set. MIB $25-40.

FT5002 Joint Action
Ghidrah. $50-70.

FT5001 Joint
Action Godzilla
(still in package).
$50-70.

IMS

FT3001	Godzilla Monster Army	
	(1991 SD set w/ 20 figures: Godzilla, Angilas, Mothra	
	(adult & larva), Rodan, King Ghidora, Minya, Kamakiras,	
	Baragon, Gorosaurus, Gabara, Hedora, Gigan, Megalon,	
	MechaGodzilla, King Seesar, Titanosaurus, Biollante,	
	Godzilla 1991 and MechaKing Ghidora)	set $25-40
FT3002	Godzilla Monster Army (Part 2)	
	(MechaKing Ghidora (w/Machine Hand), Kameba, Manda,	
	Jet Jaguar, MechaniKong, Drat, Godzillasaurus,	
	Biollante, Magma, Mogera)	set 15-20
	the above sets were also available as individual capsules	ea. 1-2

Marusan

FT4001	Balloon Blowing Baragon	$200-300
FT4002	Balloon Blowing Godzilla	300-400
FT4003	Hatching Minya	1,200-2,000
FT4004	Wind-up Godzilla	200-300

Popy

FT5001	Joint Action Godzilla (1978)	$50-70
FT5002	Joint Action Ghidrah	50-70
FT5003	Jumbosaurus Talking Godzilla (1978)	600-900
FT5004	Monster Eraser Assortment (1" tall, 1979)	
	(Godzilla, Baragon, Ghidrah, Gigan, MechaGodzilla (orig.),	
	and Rodan)	ea. 4-8

Above: FT5003 Jumbosaurus Talking Godzilla w/box. MIB 600-900.

Right: FT5003 Jumbosaurus Talking Godzilla (close-up).

FT6002 DX Combat Joe w/ box. MIB $600-800.

FT6006 sparking figures. Left to Right: Minya, Angilas, King Ghidrah, Gigan, Baragon, MechaGodzilla, and Godzilla. Each $12-16.

Wind-up egg series. Left to Right: FT6012 King Ghidrah, $35-50. FT6013 Mothra, $40-55. FT6011 Godzilla, $15-25. FT6014 Rodan, $30-45.

Takara

FT6001	Combat Joe	$300-450
FT6002	DX Combat Joe	600-800
FT6003	Gokeigen Godzilla	50-80
B-Daman Series		
FT6004	Godzilla	$8-15
FT6005	SpaceGodzilla	8-15
Sparkies (2" rolling, sparking figures)		
FT6006	Godzilla, Angilas, Baragon, Gigan, King Ghidora, MechaGodzilla, Minya	ea. 12-16
Wind-up Egg Series		
FT6011	Godzilla	$15-25
FT6012	King Ghidrah	35-50
FT6013	Mothra	40-55
FT6014	Rodan	30-45

TimeHouse

FT6015	Godzilla w/Action Figure)	$175-250

Tomy

FT7001	Batcom Godzilla (1992)	$15-25
FT7002	Batcom Ghidrah (1992)	15-25
FT7003	Batcom Rodan (1992)	15-25
FT7004	Batcom Battle Set (Godzilla & Ghidrah) (1993)	35-50
FT7005	Godzilla wind-up swimmer (1993)	8-14
FT7006	Xeron Godzilla set (figure maker w/ Godzilla, Angilas and Mothra)	20-30

Yamakatsu

FT8001	Godzilla (4" rubber figure, 1979)	$45-65
FT8002	King Ghidrah (4" rubber figure, 1979) (the above two figures were premiums from special packs of trading cards)	45-65
FT8003	Godzilla (1" rubber figures in packs, 1984) (Godzilla, Hedora, Varan, Mothra (larva), Ganime, Baragon, Gigan, MechaGodzilla, Ghidrah, Minya, Kamakiras, Rodan, and Ebirah)	ea. 2-4
FT8004	Godzilland Felt Figure (2 1/2" tall) Godzilla, Mothra, Ghidora	ea. 8-15
FT8005	Godzilland 2" Rubber Figures (Godzilla, Baragon, Ebirah, MechaGodzilla (original), Mogera)	ea. 12-20
FT8006	Godzilla Squeaking Figure (2 1/2")	10-15
FT8007	Godzilla SD Squeaking Figure (1 1/2")	8-14
FT8008	Monster Giant Gummi Set (2" tall) (Godzilla, Baragon, Gigan, Hedorah, MechaGodzilla (orig.), and Rodan)	set 25-40
FT8009	Monster Rollers (1" tall) (Godzilla, Angilas, Gigan, Ghidrah, MechaGodzilla (orig.), Rodan)	ea. 5-10
FT8010	Monster Stamps (1" tall) (Godzilla, Angilas, Gigan, Ghidrah, MechaGodzilla (orig.), and Rodan)	ea. 4-8

FT6015 Timehouse Godzilla with action figure. MIB $175-250.

FT7004 Batcom battle set with Godzilla
and King Ghidrah. MIB $35-50.

FT7003 Batcom Rodan. MIP $15-25.

FT7006 Xeron Godzilla mold
maker set. MIB $20-30.

FT8002 King
Ghidrah rubber
figure. $45-65.
FT8001 Godzilla
rubber figure.
$45-65.

FT9005 Godzilla Kaiju Dai Shuku
series part one box set. MIB $20-30.

Yutaka

FT9001	Godzilla Caricature (1995 3" SD Godzilla)	$6-12
FT9002	Godzilla Confrontation Set (1992)	
	(two sets: set one-Godzilla w/Battra adult, set two-Godzilla	
	w/ Mothra adult)	ea. 20-30
FT9003	Godzilla Real Color Series (1 1/2" rubber figures in packs, 80s)	
	(Godzilla, Megalon, Angilas, Gabara, Minya, King Seesar,	
	Varan, Titanosaurus)	ea. 2-4
FT9004	Godzilla Variety Set (1992-1995)	
	(seven rubber monsters with six milk caps)	12-18
FT9005	Godzilla Kaiju Dai Shuku	
	(deformation compilation) (Part 1)	
	(4" plastic Godzilla w/seven 1 1/2" rubber monsters)	20-30
FT9006	Godzilla Kaiju Dai Shuku (deformation	
	compilation) (Part 2, 1992)	
	(4" plastic Godzilla and King Ghidrah)	20-30
FT9008	Godzilla Kaiju Dai Shuku (Part 4, 1993)	
	(3" plastic Godzilla, Battra, King Ghidra, MechaGodzilla,	
	& Mothra)	20-30
FT9009	Godzilla Kaiju Dai Shoku (Part 6, 1994)	
	(4" plastic Godzilla and SpaceGodzilla)	16-25
FT9010	Godzilla Kaiju Dai Shuku (Part 7, 1994)	
	(2" plastic Godzilla and Space Godzilla	
	w/ eight 1" plastic figures: Rodan 1993, Mothra larva,	
	Baby Godzilla, Angilas, King Ghidora, MechaGodzilla 1993,	
	Gabara and Titanosaurus)	16-25
FT9011	Godzilla Big Variety Assortment	
	(4" Godzilla 1995, w/seven 1 1/2"	
	rubber monsters; Godzilla, SpaceGodzilla, Destroyer,	
	Baragon, Rodan, MechaKing Ghidora, MechaGodzilla '93)	16-25
FT9012	Godzilla Pocket Heroes (1993)	
	(1 1/2" rubber set, w/Godzilla, Baragon, Gigan, King Ghidora,	
	MechaGodzilla, Mothra (larva), and Rodan)	18-25
FT9013	MechaGodzilla Big Variety Assortment	
	(4" MechaGodzilla 1993 w/seven 1 1/2" rubber figures:	
	Rodan 1993, Godzilla 1993, Baby Godzilla, Gigan,	
	MechaGodzilla 1993, Baragon and MechaKing Ghidora)	20-30
FT9014	SD Godzilla Part 1 (Pocket Heroes, 1992)	
	(Godzilla 1992, King Ghidora, Mothra (adult & larva))	set 15-25
FT9015	SD Godzilla Part 2 (Pocket Heroes, 1992)	
	(Godzilla 1962, Godzilla 1991, MechaKing Ghidora,	
	MechaGodzilla)	set 15-25
FT9016	SD Godzilla Set (Pocket Heroes, 1995)	
	(Godzilla, Destroyer, King Ghidora, Little Godzilla and	
	Space Godzilla)	set 15-25
FT9017	Tataka Godzilla Set (1995)	
	(2" Burning Godzilla and Destroyer w/ 1" rubber Super XII	
	and Tank)	16-22
FT9018	Godzilla Real Hero Series (4" vinyl figures)	
	Godzilla, SpaceGodzilla, Godzilla (burning), and	
	Destroyer (final form)	ea. 6-12
FT9019	Godzilla Surfing Globe (1994)	25-40

FT9006 and 9008 Godzilla Kaiju Dai Shuku
parts two and four. MIB each $20-30.

FT9010 and 9011 Godzilla Kaiju Dai Shuku
part six and seven. MIB each $16-25.

FT9012 and 9004 Godzilla Pocket Heroes Set. MIB $18-25.
Godzilla Variety Set (1995 version). MIB $12-18.

FT9015 and 9016
Godzilla SD sets. MIB
each $15-25.

Left to Right: PT1006 Rodan $35-50. PT1001 Godzilla $20-30.
PT1004 King Ghidrah $40-60. PT1009 Mothra (adult) $20-30.
PT1003 Baragon $35-50. PT1015 Godzilla $40-60.

PT2010-2014
Godzilla live set.
Clockwise from top
left: Godzilla,
Rodan, Gigan, King
Ghidrah and
Mothra. Each $7-14.

PT5006-5009 Clock toys. Left to Right: SpaceGodzilla,
King Ghidrah, Destroyer and Godzilla. Each $22-35.

PT5021 Ghidrah sleeper and
Godzilla sleeper. Each $16-22.

MISCELLANEOUS TOYS

MT1001	Godzilla Bendie, 3" (GLJ, 1978)		$12-22
MT1002	Godzilla Bendie, 4" (GLJ, 1978)		15-25
MT1003	Godzilla Tonkachi Gao ('bopper toy') (Takara 1991)		14-22
MT1004	Godzilla on Skateboard (Hang Yip, 1990)		4-8
MT1005	Super X, vinyl toy (1984, Nitto)		65-85

PLUSH TOYS

Bandai

PT1001	Godzilla (6", 1984) (petit amour)		$20-30
PT1002	Godzilla (8", 1984) (petit amour)		22-32
PT1003	Baragon (10", 1984) (petit amour)		35-50
PT1004	King Ghidrah (10", 1984) (petit amour)		40-60
PT1005	Mothra larva (15", 1984) (petit amour)		35-50
PT1006	Rodan (10", 1984) (petit amour)		35-50
PT1007	Mothra (adult) (12", 1984) (petit amour)		40-60
PT1008	Mothra adult (8", 1993)		20-30
PT1009	Mothra (larva) (8", 1993)		32-45
PT1010	Rodan'93 (9")		35-50
PT1011	King Ghidora (8", 1993)		30-40
PT1012	New Godzilla (9", 1993)		35-50
PT1013	MechaGodzilla'93 (9", 1993)		40-60
PT1014	Godzilla, 'Fighting' (13", 1993)		65-85
PT1015	Godzilla, Action (12", 1984)		40-60
PT1016	Godzilla, Talking (12", 1985)		45-65
PT1017	Godzilla Matsui (1994)		16-25

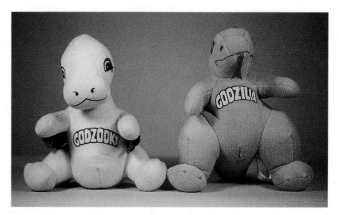

PT7002 Stuffed Godzooky. $40-50. PT7001
Stuffed Godzilla. $30-40.

Banpresto

PT2001	Godzilla (1991, 5" tall, GO-1)	$12-18
PT3003	Godzilla w/tower/plane/building (all 1993, 6" tall, VGO-3)	14-20
PT2003	Mothra larva (6", 1991, GO-3)	12-18
PT2004	King Ghidora (4", 1991 GO-4)	12-18
PT2007	Godzilla (1992, 6" tall, GO-7)	14-20
PT2015	Godzilla Bean Bag (5" tall, 1994, GO-15)	14-20
PT2016	Rodan Bean Bag (5" tall, 1994, GO-16)	14-20
PT2017	King Ghidora Bean Bag (5" tall, 1994, GO-17)	14-20
PT2018	MechaGodzilla 1993 (5" tall, 1994, GO-18)	12-18
PT2019	Mothra larva (5" tall, 1994, GO-19)	12-18
PT2025	Godzilla table cover (5", 1995 GO-25)	9-15
PT2026	Godzilla table wrap (5", 1995 GO-26)	9-15
PT2027	Godzilla door cover (5", 1995, GO-27)	10-16
PT2028	King Ghidora curtain wrap (5", 1995, GO-28)	10-16
PT2029	Mothra adult curtain wrap (5", 1995, GO-29)	10-16
PT2030	Mothra larva curtain wrap (5", 1995, GO-30)	10-16
PT4001	Godzilla (machine prize, 1994)	12-18
PT4002	MechaGodzilla (machine prize, 1994)	12-18
PT4003	Godzilla (6" w/ tower, 1994)	14-20
PT4004	Godzilla (14", 1994)	35-50

Bopper Set (1994)

PT5001/5	Godzilla (HG-1), Baby Godzilla (HG-2), King Ghidora (HG-4), MechaGodzilla 1993 (HG-5), Rodan (HG-3)	ea.$ 8-15

	Godzilla Clock Set (1995)	
PT5006/11	(each 8" tall) Godzilla, King Ghidora, SpaceGodzilla, Burning Godzilla, Godzilla Jr., Destroyer	ea. 22-35
	Godzilla Live Set (1993)	
PT2010/14	(each 6" tall) Godzilla (on guitar, GO-10), Ghidrah (on keyboards, GO-12), Gigan (on guitar, GO-13), Mothra (on saxophone, GO-14) & Rodan (on drums, GO-11)	ea. 7-14
	Newborn Set (1996)	
PT5012/16	(each 6" tall) Godzilla (NB-G1), Ghidrah (NB-G2), Mothra (NB-G4), Rodan (NB-G3), SpaceGodzilla (NB-G5)	12-18
	Roaring Set (1996)	
PT5017/19	(each 6" tall) Godzilla (OG-1), King Ghidora (OG-2), Mothra (OG-3)	ea. 14-20
	Sleepers (1993)	
PT5020/21	(each 7" long) Godzilla on pillow (HG-1), Ghidrah on pillow (HG-2)	ea. 16-22

Takara

PT6001	Godzilla plush purse (14" tall)	$25-40
PT6002	Godzilla Dekigen (wags tail, 1991)	5-10

Knickerbocker

PT7001	Godzilla (1978)	$30-40
PT7002	Godzooky (1978)	40-50

TT1001 and TT1002 Godzilla tin wind-ups. MIB $90-130 (brown), $100-150 (green).

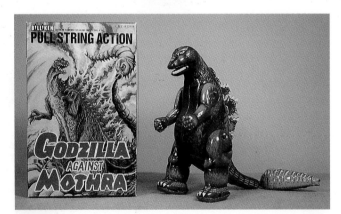

TT1003 Godzilla against Mothra tin wind-up. MIB $90-130.

TT1004 Mothra tin wind-up. MIB $60-90.

TIN TOYS

Always a favorite among collectors. The tin toys released in the Godzilla line are well designed and executed. One could only hope that companies keep up the quality and continue to release items as pleasing to the eyes as these.

Billiken

		Loose	Boxed
TT1001	Godzilla (brown) wind-up	$60	$90-130
TT1002	Godzilla (green) wind-up	70	100-150
TT1003	Godzilla against Mothra wind-up	60	90-130
TT1004	Mothra wind-up	40	60-90

Bullmark

First released in 1971, the Baragon and Godzilla were re-releases of the old Marusan molds, while the Gigan was a totally new release in 1972.

		Loose	Boxed
TT1005	Baragon (art box)	$700-800	$1000-1200
TT1006	Baragon (photo box)	700-800	900-1100
TT1007	Gigan (art box)	1200-1500	2500-3000*
TT1008	Godzilla (art box)	600-700	900-1200
TT1009	Godzilla (photo box)	600-700	800-1000

Marusan

The legendary electronic walking, wire controlled toys of the 1960s. Although not the most valuable of the Godzilla collectibles, they certainly are some of the most desired. Their size and craftsmanship makes them a favorite among toy collectors.

		Loose	Boxed
TT1010	Baragon	$900-1100	$1500-2000
TT1011	Godzilla	800-1000	1500-2000

Above: TT1005 Tin wire-controlled Baragon. Loose $700-800.

Right: Art style box for TT1005 Baragon. MIB $1,000-1,200.

Above: TT1009 Tin wire control Godzilla. Loose $600-700.

Right: TT1007 Tin Wire Control Gigan. Loose $1,200-1,500. With box $2,500-3,000.

VINYL TOYS

These are the most popular and widely collected of all Godzilla items. Vinyl Godzilla toys have been popular with kids and collectors alike for 30 years and show no signs of slowing down. In this section, we have listed all items by year of release, then alphabetical within those years.

Marusan

VT0001	Godzilla (dark blue)	1966	$250-400
VT0002	Godzilla (dark green)	1966	350-500
VT0003	Mothra (dark, gold eyes)	1966	250-400
VT0004	Mothra (lighter, silver eyes)	1966	350-500
VT0005	Baragon	1966	200-300
VT0006	Ebirah (dark red, blue)	1966	300-450
VT0007	Giant Gorilla (King Kong)	1967	1500-2500*
VT0008	MechaniKong	1967	300-450
VT0009	Gorosaurus	1967	250-400
VT0010	Gorosaurus (cream belly)	1967	350-600
VT0011	Minya (red-small)	1967	600-1000
VT0012	Minya (green-small)	1967	400-800

VT0001 Godzilla (blue version)
by Marusan. $250-400.

Above: VT0004 Mothra (lighter colored) by Marusan. $350-500.

Right: VT0005 Baragon by Marusan. $200-300.

Above: VT0006 Ebirah by Marusan (note paint on feelers). $300-450.

Right: VT0007 Giant Gorilla by Marusan. $1,500-2,500.

Far left: VT0009 Gorosaurus by Marusan. $250-400.

Left: VT0012 Minya (green version) by Marusan. $400-800.

Below: VT1002 Godzilla (dark blue version) by Bullmark. $150-250.

Bullmark

VT1001	Godzilla (light blue)	1970	$250-450
VT1002	Godzilla (dark blue)	1970	150-250
VT1003	Godzilla (sm. blue or brown)	1975	75-125
VT1004	Godzilla (med. blue or brown)	1971	125-200
VT1005	Godzilla (med. dark brown)	1971	100-200
VT1006	Godzilla (Giant size)	1970	450-900
VT1007	Angilas	1970	225-350
VT1008	Angilas (sm. green)	1971	75-125
VT1009	Rodan	1970	275-425
VT1010	Rodan (sm. pink)	1971	75-150
VT1011	Mogera (blue/green)	1970	175-300
VT1012	Mogera (green/orange)	1970	225-350
VT1013	Varan (all colors)	1970	225-350
VT1014	Mothra	1970	200-325
VT1015	Mothra (larva)	1975	100-350
VT1016	King Ghidrah	1970	90-200
VT1017	King Ghidrah (sm. w/green or blue)	1975	50-125
VT1018	King Ghidrah (med. orange/green)	1971	125-200
VT1019	King Ghidrah (med. orange/blue)	1971	100-200
VT1020	King Ghidrah (Giant size)	1970	400-800
VT1021	Baragon	1970	150-250
VT1022	Baragon (Giant size)	1971	400-800
VT1023	Ebirah (no Bullmark logo)	1970	200-350
VT1024	MechaniKong	1970	150-275
VT1025	Gorosaurus	1970	150-275
VT1026	Gorosaurus (red/blue belly)	1970	225-375
VT1027	Minya	1969	150-250
VT1028	Gabara (w/Marusan stamp on foot)	1969	150-250
VT1029	Gabara (w/Bullmark stamp on foot)	1970	175-275
VT1030	Gezora	1970	200-400
VT1031	Ganime	1970	200-350
VT1032	Kameba	1970	200-350
VT1033	Hedorah (yellow)	1971	300-500
VT1034	Hedorah (pink)	1971	1000-1500*
VT1035	Hedorah (small)	1971	175-275
VT1036	Gigan (blue/red)	1972	175-350
VT1037	Gigan (green/red)	1973	350-600
VT1038	Gigan (sm.)	1972	100-200
VT1039	Gigan (med.)	1972	80-175
VT1040	Megalon (green)	1973	1000-2000*
VT1041	Megalon (reddish-brown)	1973	1200-2000*
VT1042	Megalon (small)	1973	300-700
VT1043	Jet Jaguar	1973	600-1000
VT1044	Jet Jaguar (small)	1973	150-300
VT1045	MechaGodzilla	1974	1200-2000*
VT1046	MechaGodzilla (small gray)	1975	75-150
VT1047	MechaGodzilla (small green)	1975	150-300
VT1048	MechaGodzilla (medium gray)	1974	50-90
VT1049	MechaGodzilla (medium green)	1974	75-150
VT1050	Titanosaurus	1975	200-400

Above: Left to Right: VT1003 Small brown Godzilla, $75-125. VT1004 Medium blue Godzilla, $125-200. VT1003 Small blue Godzilla, $75-125. All by Bullmark.

Right: VT1006 Giant Size Godzilla (w/tower). $450-900.

Above: VT1008 Small Angilas (front and back) by Bullmark. Each $75-125.

Left: VT1007 Angilas by Bullmark. $225-350.

VT1009 Rodan
by Bullmark.
$275-425.

Far left: Left to
Right: VT1012
Green/orange
version Mogera
(front). $225-350.
VT1011 Blue/green
version Mogera
(back). $175-300.

Left: VT1010 Small
Rodan by
Bullmark. 75-150.

VT1013 Varan
(front and back)
by Bullmark. Each
$225-350.

Above: VT1015 Small Mothra (larva) by Bullmark. $100-350.

Left: VT1014 Mothra (adult form) by Bullmark. $200-325.

VT1016 King Ghidrah by Bullmark. $90-200.

VT1017 Small King Ghidrah (w/blue highlights), $50-125.
VT1019 Medium King Ghidrah (w/blue neck), $100-200.

VT1020 Giant size King Ghidrah by Bullmark (notice open mouths). $400-800.

Above: VT1021 Baragon (standard size). $150-250.

Right: VT1022 Giant size Baragon with tower (notice wide open mouth). $400-800.

VT1023 Ebirah (front and back) by Bullmark. (No paint on tentacles). $200-350.

136

Above: VT1026 Gorosaurus (back) and VT1025 Gorosaurus (front). VT1025 price $150-275.

Left: VT1024 MechaniKong by Bullmark. $150-275.

Above: VT1027 Minya by Bullmark. $150-250.

Left: Close up of VT1026 Gorosaurus showing colors on belly. $225-375.

Comparison of Bullmark Minya (VT1027) and
Marusan Minya (VT0012) showing size difference.

VT1028 Bullmark Gabara with Marusan
stamp on foot. $150-250. Please note,
although some Gabara's have the
Marusan stamp on their foot, all were
produced by Bullmark.

Above: VT1031 Ganime
by Bullmark. $200-350.

Left: VT1030 Gezora by
Bullmark. $200-400.

VT1032 Kameba (front and back of different color variations) by Bullmark. Each $200-350.

Above: VT1035 Small Hedorah (front and back) by Bullmark. Each $175-275.

Left: VT1033 Yellow Hedorah by Bullmark. $300-500.

Back of VT1037 Gigan (green/red version) and front of VT1036 Gigan (blue/red version). Price for VT1036, $175-350.

Above: VT1039 Medium Gigan, $80-175. VT1038 Small Gigan, $100-200.

Left: VT1037 Gigan (red/green variation) front view. $350-600.

Above: VT1042 Front and back view of small Megalon. Each $300-700.

Left: VT1041 Reddish brown standard size Megalon. $1,200-2,000.

VT1043 Bagged and unbagged large size Jet Jaguar. Unbagged $600-1,000. Bagged $-??

VT1044 Bagged small Jet Jaguar. Unbagged price $150-300. Bagged $250-450.

141

VT1045 MechaGodzilla standard size by Bullmark. $1,200-2,000.

VT1045 Side view of MechaGodzilla.

VT1048 Medium gray MechaGodzilla. $50-90.
VT1047 Small green MechaGodzilla. $150-300.
VT1049 Medium green MechaGodzilla. $75-150.

Close-up of small
MechaGodzilla
(VT1047). $150-300.

VT1050 Bullmark
Titanosaurus.
$200-400.

VT2002 Popy Baragon (green and
black versions). Each $80-160.

Popy

VT2001	Godzilla (attacking)	1978	$60-150
VT2101	Godzilla (attacking, no silver paint)	1978	75-175
VT2002	Baragon	1978	80-160
VT2003	Gigan	1978	90-175
VT2004	Ghidrah	1978	80-150
VT2005	MechaGodzilla	1978	80-150
VT2006	Rodan	1978	80-160
VT2007	Godzilla (Giant Red)	1979	150-300
VT2008	Godzilla (lg.)	1979	125-250
VT2009	Godzilla (md.)	1979	75-175
VT2010	Godzilla (sm.)	1979	30-60

VT2003 Gigan $90-175.
VT2004 Ghidrah $80-150.
VT2005 MechaGodzilla
$80-150. All by Popy.

Above: VT2006 Popy Rodan (silver and black versions). Each $80-160.

Right: VT2007 Giant Red Godzilla by Popy. $150-300.

Comparison of Beetland Godzilla bank (BN1001) and Popy giant red Godzilla (VT2007).

VT2009 Godzilla (medium size) $75-175. VT2010 Godzilla (small size) $30-60. VT2008 Godzilla (large size) $125-250.

VT3002 Godzilla (silver fin version) $25-50. VT3003 Godzilla (small silver fin version) $10-20. VT3004 Godzilla (small gold fin version) $10-20. VT3001 Godzilla (gold fin version) $30-60.

Yamakatsu

VT3001	Godzilla (gold fins)	1983	$30-60
VT3002	Godzilla (silver fins)	1983	25-50
VT3003	Godzilla (sm., silver fins)	1983	10-20
VT3004	Godzilla (sm., gold fins)	1983	10-20
VT3005	Baragon	1983	40-70
VT3006	Angilas	1983	30-60
VT3007	King Ghidrah	1983	50-100
VT3008	MechaGodzilla	1983	25-50
VT3009	Mothra	1983	40-80
VT3010	MechaniKong	1983	30-60

VT3005-3007 Yamakatsu figures of Baragon $40-70, Angilas $30-60, and King Ghidrah $50-100.

VT3008-3010 Yamakatsu MechaGodzilla $25-50, Mothra larva $40-80, and MechaniKong $30-60.

VT4001 Bandai
Godzilla 1962
style. $100-175.

Bandai

VT4001	Godzilla (1962 style)	1983	$125-225
VT4002	Godzilla (1964 style)	1984	60-100
VT4003	Godzilla (1964 repaint)	1989	50-80
VT4004	Godzilla (1984 style)	1984	90-175
VT4005	King Ghidrah	1984	90-175
VT4006	King Ghidrah (1988 repaint)	1988	75-150
VT4007	MechaGodzilla (larger)	1984	60-125
VT4008	MechaGodzilla (smaller)	1988	50-90
VT4009	Godzilla (great monsters series)	1984	175-250
VT4010	Godzilla (above, smaller re-release)	1988	125-200
VT4011	Godzilla (g.m.series-bronze)	1984	250-400
VT4012	King Ghidrah (g.m.series)	1984	200-325
VT4013	Mothra (g.m.series)	1984	60-100
VT4014	Gigan	1989	27-45
VT4015	Angilas	1989	24-40
VT4016	Mothra (sm. larva)	1989	9-15
VT4017	Megalon	1990	60-100
VT4018	Rodan	1990	50-90
VT4019	King Ghidora (1991 style)	1991	24-40
VT4020	Mothra (large larva)	1991	18-30
VT4021	Mecha King Ghidora	1991	80-140
VT4022	Godzilla (1991 closed mouth)	1991	75-125
VT4023	Godzilla (larger size)	1992	90-150
VT4024	Mothra (1964 style adult)	1992	60-100
VT4025	Minya	1992	40-75
VT4026	Biollante	1992	150-250
VT4027	Baragon	1992	125-175
VT4028	MechaniKong	1992	40-60
VT4029	Godzilla (open mouth)	1992	24-40
VT4030	Mothra (larva new style)	1992	80-150
VT4031	Mothra (adult new style)	1992	24-40
VT4032	Battra (larva)	1992	40-75

Above: VT4002 1964 style
Godzilla original version. $45-80.

Above right: VT4003 1964 style
Godzilla, 1989 repainted version.
Note darker gray base paint, and
more silver highlights. $40-70.

Right: VT4004 1984 style
Godzilla. $90-150.

Comparison of sizes of the first three Bandai vinyl Godzillas. (Left to Right: 1984, 1964, 1962).

Above: Comparison of VT4005 King Ghidrah (on left) and VT4006 King Ghidrah (on right). Slightly darker paints and highlights on original.

Left: VT4005 Original style King Ghidrah figure. $90-150.

VT4008 Smaller 1988 version of original MechaGodzilla ($50-90) on left, compared to slightly larger original VT4007 version MechaGodzilla on right ($60-100).

VT4033	Battra (adult)	1992	24-40
VT4034	Godzillasaurus	1993	20-40
VT4134	Godzilla 1991/Godzillasaurus 2-pack	1993	200-250
VT4035	Gorosaurus	1993	45-75
VT4036	Hedorah	1993	30-50
VT4037	Kamakiras	1993	25-45
VT4038	King Caesar	1993	15-25
VT4039	King Kong	1993	15-25
VT4040	Jet Jaguar	1993	15-25
VT4041	MechaGodzilla (1993 style)	1993	25-40
VT4042	Fire Rodan	1993	25-40
VT4043	Baby Godzilla		20-30
VT4044	Mogera		20-35
VT4045	SpaceGodzilla	1994	50-90
VT4046	Little Godzilla	1994	40-80
VT4047	G-Force Mogera	1994	20-35
VT4048	Super Premium Godzilla	1994	250-400
VT4049	Destroyer (crab form)	1995	20-35
VT4050	Destroyer (final form)	1995	20-35
VT4051	Godzilla Jr.	1995	12-20
VT4052	Burning Godzilla	1995	18-30
VT4053	Theater Burning Godzilla ("meltdown")	1995	60-100
VT4054	Super Final Premium Godzilla	1995	300-500
VT4055	Memorial Box Set	1996	350-600

VT4009 Great Monster Series 1964 style Godzilla (about 18" tall). $160-240.

VT4011 Limited Bronze version of the Great Monster Series Godzilla. $250-400.

Slightly smaller 1988 re-release of Great Monster Series Godzilla (VT4010, $120-200) on left, compared to original version on right.

VT4012 Great Monster Series King Ghidrah (about 14" tall).
Note wings to detach from body. $200-325.

VT4013 Great Monster Series Mothra
larva (about 12" long). $60-100.

VT4015 Angilas vinyl figure. $27-40.

VT4014 Bandai Gigan. $27-45.

VT4017 Megalon figure
by Bandai. $60-100.

VT4018 Bandai Rodan. $50-90.

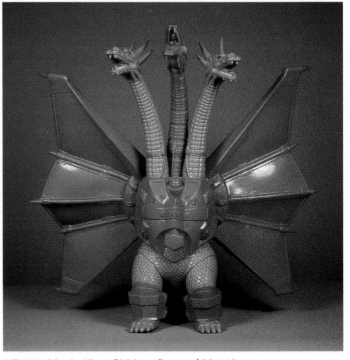

VT4019 New style King Ghidora (note
horns on side of head). $24-40.

VT4021 MechaKing Ghidora figure. $80-140.

VT4022 Godzilla 1991 style figure
(note closed mouth). $75-125.

VT4023 Large size (14" tall) 1991
style Godzilla figure. $90-150.

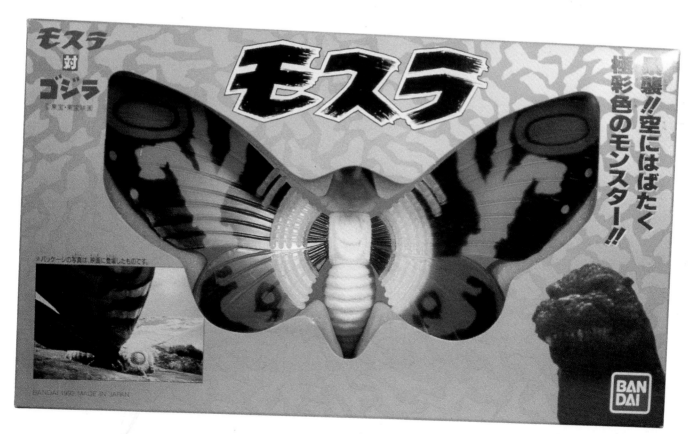

VT4024 Adult Mothra 1964 style
figure still in box. MIB $60-100.

VT4025 Minya (Godzilla's son)
figure. $40-75.

VT4026 Biollante figure (out of box).
MIB $150-250.

VT4027 Baragon figure. $125-175.

VT4028 MechaniKong figure. $40-60.

VT4030 Mothra larva, new 1992 style. $80-150.

Comparison of all four Mothra larvae. Clockwise from top right: VT4030 1992 style Mothra larva ($80-150), VT4016 small Mothra larva ($9-15), VT4020 large Mothra larva ($18-30), and VT4013 Great Monster Series Mothra larva ($60-100).

VT4033 Battra adult in box ($24-40),

VT4031 Mothra adult in box ($24-40).

Clockwise from top right: VT4033 Battra adult ($24-40), VT4030 Mothra 1992 larva ($80-150), VT4032 Battra larva ($40-75), and VT4031 Mothra 1992 adult ($24-40).

VT4034 Godzillasaurus. $20-40.

VT4134 Godzillasaurus and Godzilla
(1991 style) two-pack. MIP $200-250.

VT4035 Gorosaurus figure. $45-75.

VT4036 Hedorah figure. $30-50.

VT4037 Kamakiras
figure. $25-45.

VT4038 King Caesar figure. $15-25.

VT4039 King Kong figure. $15-25.

Above: VT4042 Fire Rodan figure. $25-40.

Left: VT4043 Baby Godzilla. $20-30.

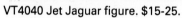
VT4040 Jet Jaguar figure. $15-25.

Group shot of VT4038 King Caesar ($15-25), VT4044 Mogera ($20-35),
VT4040 Jet Jaguar ($15-25), and VT4039 King Kong ($15-25).

Above: VT4045 Space Godzilla figure. $50-90.

Above right: VT4046 Little Godzilla figure. $40-80.

Right: VT4047 G-Force Mogera. $20-35.

VT4049 Destroyer (crab or early form). $20-35.

VT4050 Destroyer final form figure. $20-35.

VT4052 Burning
Godzilla figure. $18-30.

VT4053 Theater Burning
Godzilla ("meltdown",
limited to 5000). $60-100.

VT4054 Super Final Premium Godzilla
(limited to 4000). $300-500.

Individual Figures:

VT4056	Godzilla (1962 style)	$50-80
VT4057	Angilas	20-35
VT4058	Battra (larva)	20-35
VT4059	G-Force Mogera	18-30
VT4060	Ghidrah (1964 style)	30-55
VT4061	Gigan	20-35
VT4062	Godzillasaurus	14-20
VT4063	Hedorah	20-35
VT4064	MechaGodzilla (1974 style)	30-55
VT4065	MechaGodzilla (1993 style)	18-30
VT4066	Megalon	40-60
VT4067	Mothra (larva)	8-15
VT4068	Rodan (1956 style)	30-55
VT4069	SpaceGodzilla	40-60
VT4070	Godzilla Forever Set (1996)	350-550

VT4055 Group Shot of figures from the
Godzilla Memorial Box. Set $350-600.

VT4057
Memorial box
Angilas (on left)
and VT4015
Angilas (on
right).

VT4060 Memorial Box Ghidrah (on left)
and VT4006 Ghidrah (on right).

VT4014 Gigan (on left) and VT4061
Memorial Box Gigan (on right)

VT4034 Godzillasaurus (on left) and VT4062
Memorial Box Godzillasaurus on right.

VT4063 Memorial Box Hedorah (on left)
and VT4036 Hedorah on right.

VT4008 MechaGodzilla on left and VT4064
Memorial Box MechaGodzilla on right.

VT4041 MechaGodzilla on left and
VT4065 MechaGodzilla on right.

VT4066 Memorial Box Megalon
and VT4017 Megalon on right.

VT4018 Rodan on left and VT4068
Memorial Box Rodan on right.

VT4069 Memorial Box
Space Godzilla on left
and VT4045 Space
Godzilla on right.

Above: VT4070
Godzilla Forever Set
group set. $350-550.

Left: VT4001 Original
1962 style Godzilla
and VT4056 Memorial
Box Godzilla.

Individual Figures:

VT4071	Godzilla 1962 Upgrade Version	$70-110
VT4072	Godzilla 1993 Final Version	70-110
VT4073	Godzilla 1995 Meltdown Version	70-110
VT4074	Baby Godzilla Upgrade Version	30-50
VT4075	Fire Rodan Upgrade Version	40-60
VT4076	MechaKing Ghidora Upgrade Version	60-100

VT4072 Godzilla 1993 final version
Forever series figure. $70-110.

VT4073 Godzilla 1995 Meltdown version
Forever series figure. $70-110.

VT4074 Forever version Baby Godzilla ($30-50) and VT4043 Baby Godzilla.

VT4042 Fire Rodan and VT4075 Forever version Fire Rodan. $40-60.

VT4021 MechaKing Ghidora and VT4076 Forever version MechaKing Ghidora. $60-100.

Tag for Bandai re-issue Bullmark figures.

Bandai Re-issue Bullmark Figures

All made from original molds with new paint jobs.

VT4501	Godzilla	$35-55
VT4502	Angilas	35-55
VT4503	Rodan	35-55
VT4504	Mothra	35-55
VT4505	King Ghidrah	30-50
VT4506	Baragon	30-50
VT4507	Minya	30-50
VT4508	Gigan	40-60
VT4509	Megalon	50-80
VT4510	MechaGodzilla	50-80

Marmit

VT6001	Godzilla 1954	1996	$40-60
VT6002	Godzilla 1954 Ltd. Blue	1996	60-100
VT6003	Godzilla 1954 Ltd. Green	1996	75-100
VT6011	Godzilla 1955	1996	40-60
VT6021	Godzilla 1962	1997	40-60
VT6031	Godzilla 1964	1997	40-60
VT6041	Baragon	1997	40-60
VT6042	Baragon Ltd. Blue	1997	60-100
VT6051	Rodan	1997	40-60
VT6052	Rodan Ltd. Blue		60-100
VT6061	Meganuron	1997	40-60
VT6062	Meganuron Ltd. Blue	1997	60-100
VT6071	Manda	1997	40-60

M-1 ichigo

VT7001	Cosmos (Mothra fairies)	1998	$40-60

VT6011 Godzilla 1955 version and VT6001
Godzilla 1954 version. Each $40-60.

VT6021 Godzilla 1962 version and VT6031
Godzilla 1964 version. Each $40-60.

VT6042 Blue Baragon, VT6052 Blue Rodan,
and VT6002 Blue Godzilla. Each $60-100.

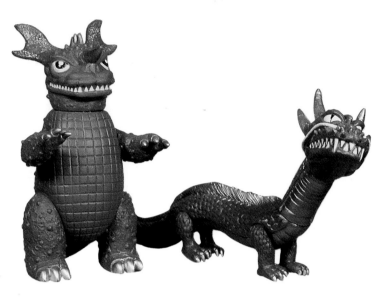

Above: VT6041 Baragon and VT6071 Manda. Each $40-60.

Left: VT6003 Limited green version of Godzilla 1954. $75-100.

UNITED STATES TOYS

Axlon
UT0101	Petster Godzilla	$100-125

Ben Cooper Toys
UT0151	Godzilla rubber figure (4")	$10-15

Carlin Playthings
UT0201	Godzilla bendable (3")	$15-22
UT0202	Godzilla bendable (4")	17-25

H.G. Toys
UT0301	Godzilla Battles the Tricephalon (1978)	$150-225

Imperial
UT0401	Bubble Blowing Godzilla (1985)	$15-25
UT0403	Godzilla (rubber 5") (1984)	4-9
UT0404	Godzilla (rubber 7") (1984)	8-15
UT0405	Godzilla (rubber 15") (1984)	15-25

Mattel
UT0501	Godzilla (Godzilla's Gang) (1978)	$60-90
UT0502	Godzilla (Shogun Warriors line) (1978)	40-70 loose, 100-140 boxed
UT0503	Rodan (1979)	70-110 loose, 200-275 boxed

MGA Entertainment
UT0601	Godzilla Virtual Reality Pet (1997)	$10-20

Trendmasters
Electronic Walkers
UT1001	Godzilla	$15-25
UT1002	Ghidorah	15-25

G-Force Figures
UT1101	Black	$4-9
UT1102	Blue	4-9
UT1103	Red	4-9
UT1104	White	4-9

Godzilla Bendables
UT1201	Godzilla	$4-8
UT1202	Supercharged Godzilla	5-10
UT1203	Biollante	5-10
UT1204	Ghidorah	4-8
UT1205	MechaGodzilla	4-8
UT1206	Moguera	5-10

UT0101 Petster Godzilla electronic toy. MIB $100-125.

UT0202 Godzilla bendable $17-25,
and UT0151 rubber Godzilla $10-15.

UT1207	Mothra	4-8
UT1208	Rodan	4-8
UT1209	SpaceGodzilla	5-10

'Godzilla Hatched' Series
(continues as 'MicroMountain Series)

UT1301	Godzilla	$4-8
UT1302	Godzilla (arms up)	5-10
UT1303	Ghidorah	4-8
UT1304	MechaGodzilla	4-8
UT1305	Mothra	4-8
UT1306	Rodan	4-8

'Godzilla vs.' Two Packs (4" figures)

UT1401	vs. Anguirus	$12-18
UT1402	vs. Battra	10-16
UT1403	vs. Biollante	10-16
UT1404	vs. Ghidora	8-14
UT1405	vs. Gigan	10-16
UT1406	vs. Mecha Ghidora	8-14
UT1407	vs. MechaGodzilla	8-14
UT1408	vs. MechaGodzilla (Thundering Godzilla)	10-16
UT1409	vs. Moguera	12-18
UT1410	vs. Mothra	8-14
UT1411	vs. Rodan	8-14
UT1412	vs. SpaceGodzilla	12-18

40th Anniversary Collectors Edition (4" figures)

UT1451	King of the Monsters Assortment	$25-40
UT1452	Godzilla Wars Assortment	25-40
UT1453	Godzilla Wars Repaint Assortment	25-40

6" Figure Series with Sound

UT1501	Godzilla	$6-10
UT1502	Supercharged Godzilla	6-10
UT1503	Baragon	15-20
UT1504	Battra	6-10
UT1505	Biollante	6-10
UT1506	Ghidorah	6-10
UT1507	Gigan	6-10
UT1508	MechaGhidorah	6-10
UT1509	MechaGodzilla	6-10
UT1510	Megalon	15-20
UT1511	Moguera	6-10
UT1512	Mothra	6-10
UT1513	Rodan	8-12
UT1514	SpaceGodzilla	6-10
UT1515	Varan	15-20

6" Figure Series without Sound

UT1601	Godzilla	$4-8
UT1602	Supercharged Godzilla	4-8
UT1603	Battra	6-10
UT1604	Biollante	6-10
UT1605	Ghidorah	4-8
UT1606	Gigan	6-10
UT1607	MechaGhidorah	4-8
UT1608	MechaGodzilla	4-8
UT1609	Moguera	6-10
UT1610	Mothra	4-8
UT1611	Rodan	6-10
UT1612	SpaceGodzilla	6-10

UT0403 Imperial 5" rubber Godzilla $4-9,
and UT0405 15" rubber Godzilla $15-25.

UT0501 Godzilla's Gang Godzilla figure
(says 'Made in Taiwan' on foot). $60-90.

10" Figure Series		
UT1701	Godzilla	$15-25
UT1702	Supercharged Godzilla	15-25
UT1703	Biollante	30-40
UT1704	Ghidorah	20-30
UT1705	Gigan	15-25
UT1706	MechaGhidorah	15-15
UT1707	MechaGodzilla	25-35
UT1708	Mothra	15-25
UT1709	Rodan	15-25
UT1710	SpaceGodzilla	15-25
Jump-Up Figures		
UT1751	Godzilla	$3-6
UT1752	MechaGodzilla	3-6
UT1753	Rodan	3-6
MicroBattle Set (all are Godzilla vs. ...)		
UT1801	Biollante in Washington D.C.	$10-17
UT1802	G-Force in Command Central	10-17
UT1803	Ghidorah in San Francisco	8-15
UT1804	MechaGodzilla in Los Angeles	8-15
UT1805	MechaGodzilla in Defense Base	10-17
UT1806	Rodan in New York	8-15
UT1805	SpaceGodzilla in Tokyo	14-20

Above: UT0502 Shogun Warrior Godzilla with box. MIB $100-140.

Right: UT0503 Mattel Rodan. MIB $200-275.

UT1001-1002 Electronic walking Godzilla and King Ghidora. MIB Each $15-25.

Godzilla Bendables. Left to Right: UT1209 Space Godzilla ($5-10), UT1203 Biollante ($5-10), UT1206 Moguera ($5-10), UT1207 Mothra ($4-8), and UT1205 MechaGodzilla ($4-8).

Godzilla Hatched series. Left to Right: UT1302 Godzilla ($5-10), UT1305 Mothra ($4-8), UT1306 Rodan ($4-8), and UT1304 MechaGodzilla ($4-8).

MicroMountain Series		
UT1901	Godzilla	$5-10
UT1902	Supercharged Godzilla	7-13
UT1903	Anguirus	9-15
UT1904	MechaGodzilla	5-10
UT1905	Moguera	9-15
UT1906	SpaceGodzilla	9-15
Miscellaneous Items		
UT2001	Bendable Godzilla Key Ring	$2-4
UT2002	Garuda Ship (Fits on 10" MechaGodzilla)	5-10
UT2003	Godzilla Attacks New York Playset	14-25
UT2004	Godzilla Bank	10-15
UT2005	Godzilla Fun Straw	4-8
UT2006	Growing Godzilla	2-4
UT2007	Godzilla Missile Blaster Set	15-25
UT2008	Godzilla Slide Puzzle	2-4
Power-up Figures		
UT2101	Godzilla	$8-15
UT2102	Anguirus	15-25
UT2103	Kumonga	15-25
UT2104	MechaGhidorah	8-15
UT2105	MechaGodzilla	8-15
UT2106	Rodan	8-15
Wind-up Walkers		
UT2201	Godzilla	$4-7
UT2202	MechaGhidorah	4-7
UT2203	MechaGodzilla	4-7

UT1452 Godzilla 40th Anniversary collector's set ($25-40), and UT1453 repainted collector's set ($25-40).

Clockwise from top left: UT2105 MechaGodzilla power-up figure ($8-15), UT1503 6" Baragon ($15-20), UT1505 6" Biollante ($6-10), UT1515 6" Varan ($15-20), UT1510 6" Megalon ($15-20), and UT2104 Power-up MechaKing Ghidora ($8-15).

UT1708 10" Mothra ($15-25) and UUT1709 10" Rodan ($15-25).

Left to Right: UT2001 Godzilla key ring ($2-4), UT2203 wind-up MechaGodzilla ($4-7), UT2006 Growing Godzilla ($2-4), and UT2008 Godzilla Slide Puzzle ($2-4).

TRADING CARDS/PHONE CARDS

Trading Cards

Amada

	Godzilla vs. King Ghidora	
TR1001	36 regular cards	$15-20
	6 prism cards	10-18
	Godzilla vs. Mothra'92	
TR1002	36 regular cards	15-20
	6 prism cards	10-18
	Godzilla vs. MechaGodzilla'93	
TR1003	36 regular cards	15-20
	6 prism cards	10-18
	Godzilla vs. SpaceGodzilla	
TR1004	36 regular cards	15-20
	6 prism cards	10-18
	Godzilla vs. Destroyer	
TR1005	36 regular cards	15-20
	6 prism cards	10-18
	Godzilla and the Giant Monsters (1992)	
TR1006	36 regular cards	15-20
	6 prism cards	10-18
	Godzilla and Toho Monsters Collection	
TR1007	90 regular cards	30-45
	2 foil cards	25-35
	Godzilla Wide Collection	
TR1008	63 regular cards	35-50
	12 Prism Cards	15-25
	6 special cards	50-80
	Trading Collection	
TC1009	102 Series Cards	25-35
	8 checklists	4-8
	4 holograms (Godzilla, Destroyer, MechaGodzilla, SpaceGodzilla)	36-50
	album w/card #103	16-28

Bandai

TR1010	Godzilla and Giant Monsters (1992)	
	36 cards	$20-25
	6 prisms	10-20
TR1011	Godzilla Battle Game Set (1992)	25-30

Banpresto

TR1012	Godzilla series (24 cards, 1992)	$35-50

Futami

TR1013	Godzilla 'Bar Code' series (80 cards, 1992)	$10-20
TR1014	Godzilla Card 100 (MechaGodzilla, 1993)	12-24
TR1015	Godzilla Card 100 (SpaceGodzilla, 1994)	12-24
TR1016	Godzilla Card 100 (Destroyer, 1995)	12-24
TR1017	Godzilla Card 100 (Toho Monsters, 1995)	12-24

Meiji

TR1018	Godzilla card series	
	30 regular cards	$30-50
	1 Godzilla Hologram card	8-12
TR1019	Godzilla Gum Card Series (1992)	
	36 cards	30-50
	6 prism cards	15-25
TR1020	Godzilla Gum card series (1993)	
	36 cards	30-50
	6 prism cards	15-25
	1 Godzilla hologram card	10-15

Morinaga

TR1021	Godzilla Chocolate Snack (1992)	
	24 cards	$18-30
TR1022	Godzilla Chocolate Snack (1993)	
	24 cards	18-30
TR1023	Godzilla Chocolate Snack (1994)	
	24 cards	18-30
TR1024	Godzilla Gum Cards #1	
	100 cards	80-100
	10 stickers	25-40
TR1025	Godzilla Gum Cards #2	
	100 cards	80-100
	10 stickers	25-40

TC1004 Godzilla vs. SpaceGodzilla prism cards. Set $10-18.

TC1006 Godzilla and the giant monster cards. Set $30-45.

TC1008 Godzilla wide collection cards. Set $35-50.

TC1009 prism cards from Trading collection. Set $25-35.

TC1013 Godzilla barcode series ($10-20), and TC1014 Godzilla card 100 ($12-24).

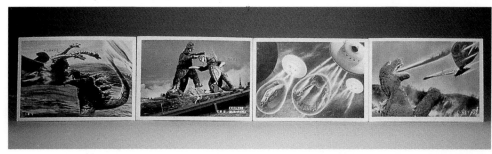

TC1032 Yamakatsu bromide cards. Each $5-11.

TC1039 Toho monsters mini-card box. Box $40-70.

Toho

TR1026	Godzilla Battle Cards Pt.1 (200 cards)	$50-80
TR1027	Godzilla Battle Cards Pt.2 (200 cards)	45-60

Toy Card Co.

TR1029	Godzilla Toy Card set 144 cards	$35-50
	6 foil cards	8-15

TV Magazine

TR1031	Godzilla Giant Monsters (40 cards)	$10-20

Yamakatsu

TR1032	Bromide Card Series (3 1/2" x 5") (1971-1973)	ea. $5-11
TR1033	Godzilla Gum Cards (1980) Series 1 and 2	each set 80-100
TR1034	Godzilla'84 mini-cards 42 cards	15-25
TR1035	Godzilla vs. the Thing Special Set 16 cards	20-30
TR1036	Godzilland Comicsaurus (1983) 42 cards	10-20

TR1037	Godzilland Stickers (card size) 42 stickers	20-25
TR1038	Godzilland Stickers (ruler size) 42 stickers	25-30
TR1039	Toho Monsters Mini-Cards (30 packs per box, 2" x 2 1/2")	40-70
TR1040	Toho Monsters Paper Collection (stickers) (50 packs per box, 1 1/2" x 2")	30-60
	Sticker Album	8-15

Phone Cards

TR2001	Godzilla vs. Biollante	$15-20
TR2002	Godzilla vs. King Ghidora (2 diff.)	ea. 15-20
TR2003	Godzilla vs. Mothra'92 (3 diff.)	ea. 12-20
TR2004	Godzilla vs. MechaGodzilla'93 (2 different)	ea. 18-25
TR2005	Godzilla vs. SpaceGodzilla (2 diff.)	ea. 10-15
TR2006	Godzilla vs. Destroyer Prism Cards (2 cards, theaters only,)	8-12
TR2007	Godzilla Telephone Card Collection (19 cards)	200-250

VIDEO & LASERDISCS

Videos

Gakken Video
VI1001	*I can Learn Hiragana* (Godzilland)	$20-25
VI1002	*Let's Count 1-2-3* (Godzilland)	20-25

Manga Live
VI1201	*Godzilla vs. King Ghidora*	$20-30
VI1202	*Godzilla vs. Mothra* (1992)	20-30

Toho Video
VI2001	*Godzilla 1954* (TG 0822 and 4287)	$30-60
VI2002	*Godzilla Raids Again* (TG 1107 and 4288)	30-60
VI2003	*King Kong Vs. Godzilla* (TG 4289)	30-60
VI2004	*Godzilla vs. Mothra* (TG 0847 and 4290)	30-60
VI2005	*Ghidrah, the Three Headed Monster* (TG 0653 and 4291)	30-60
VI2006	*Monster Zero* (TG 0632 and 4291)	30-60
VI2007	*Godzilla vs. the Sea Monster* (TG 0641 and 4293)	30-60
VI2008	*Son of Godzilla* (TG 0846 and 4294)	30-60
VI2009	*Destroy All Monsters* (TG 4295)	30-60
VI2010	*Godzilla's Revenge* (TG 1486)	30-60
VI2011	*Godzilla vs. the Smog Monster* (TG 1167)	30-60
VI2012	*Godzilla vs. Gigan* (TG 4296)	30-60
VI2013	*Godzilla vs. Megalon* (TG 1720)	30-60
VI2014	*Godzilla vs. MechaGodzilla* (TG 1181)	30-60
VI2015	*Terror of MechaGodzilla* (TG 1155)	30-60
VI2016	*Godzilla 1984* (TG 1148)	30-60
VI2116	*Godzilla 1985*-US version (TA 4015)	20-40
VI2017	*Godzilla vs. Biollante* (TG 4100)	30-60
VI2018	*Godzilla vs. King Ghidora*	30-60
VI2019	*Godzilla vs. Mothra 1992*	30-60
VI2020	*Godzilla vs. MechaGodzilla 1993*	30-60
VI2021	*Godzilla vs. SpaceGodzilla*	30-60
VI2022	*Godzilla vs. Destroyer*	30-60
VI2023	*Godzilla Fantasia* (TA 4140)	40-80
VI2024	*Godzilla vs. The Monster Army* (TA 4002)	40-80
VI2025	*Legend of Godzilla* (TA 4141)	35-70
VI2026	*Making of Godzilla 1984*	50-90
VI2028	*Toho Monster SF Encyclopedia Series #1* (TA 1247)	20-40
VI2029	*Toho Monster SF Encyclopedia Series #2* (TA 1248)	20-40
VI2030	*Toho Monster SF Encyclopedia Series #3* (TA 1260)	20-40
VI2031	*Toho Monster SF Encyclopedia Series #4* (TA 1261)	20-40
VI2032	*Toho Monster SF Encyclopedia Series #5* (TA 1265)	20-40
VI2033	*Toho Monster SF Encyclopedia Series #6* (TA 1266)	40-80
VI3034	*Toho Monster SF Encyclopedia Series #7* (TA 1267)	20-40
VI2035	*Toho Monster SF Encyclopedia Series #8* (TA 1268)	40-80
VI2036	*Toho Monster SF Encyclopedia Series #9* (TA 1269)	30-50
VI2037	*Toho Monster SF Encyclopedia Series #10* (TA 1270)	20-40
VI2038	*Toho Monster SF Encyclopedia Series #11* (TA1271)	30-50
VI2039	*Toho Monster Graffiti* (Trailers) Vol.1 (TA 1243)	40-70
VI2040	*Toho Monster Graffiti* (Trailers) Vol.2 (TA 1244)	40-70
VI2041	*Toho Unused Special Effects Clips*	50-80
VI2042	*Symphonic Godzilla vs. MechaGodzilla*	20-30

U.S. Releases
VI3001	*Bambi Meets Godzilla* (Rhino, 1987)	$10-20
VI3002	*Godzilla, King of the Monsters* (Vestron Video)	10-20
VI3003	*Godzilla, King of the Monsters* (Paramount)	5-10
VI3004	*Godzilla Raids Again* (Video Treasures)	10-20
VI3005	*King Kong vs. Godzilla* (Goodtimes)	6-12
VI3006	*Godzilla vs. Mothra* (Paramount)	8-15
VI3007	*Ghidrah, the Three Headed Monster* (Video Treasures)	10-20
VI3008	*Monster Zero* (Simitar Video)	10-20
VI3009	*Monster Zero* (Paramount)	8-15
VI3010	*Godzilla vs. the Sea Monster* (Video Treasures)	10-20
VI3011	*Godzilla vs. the Sea Monster* (Goodtimes)	8-15
VI3012	*Son of Godzilla* (Video Treasures)	10-20
VI3013	*Godzilla's Revenge* (Simitar Video)	8-15
VI3014	*Godzilla's Revenge* (Paramount Video)	8-15
VI3015	*Godzilla vs. the Smog Monster* (Orion Home Video)	15-25
VI3016	*Godzilla vs. Gigan* (New World Video)	10-20
VI3017	*Godzilla vs. Gigan* (Star Maker Video)	8-15
VI3018	*Godzilla vs. Megalon* (Goodtimes)	8-15
VI3019	*Godzilla vs. MechaGodzilla* (New World Video)	8-15
VI3020	*Godzilla vs. MechaGodzilla* (Star Maker Video)	8-15
VI3021	*Godzilla vs. CosmicMonster* (Goodtimes)	8-15
VI3022	*Godzilla vs. CosmicMonster* (United American Video)	8-15
VI3023	*Terror of MechaGodzilla* (Paramount)	8-15
VI3024	*Godzilla 1985* (New World Video)	10-20
VI3025	*Godzilla 1985* (Star Maker Video)	8-15
VI3026	*Godzilla vs. Biollante* (HBO Video)	15-25

VI101-1002 Children's learning videos. Each $20-25.

VI3004 and 3010 *Godzilla Raids Again* and *Godzilla vs. the Sea Monsters* videos. Each $10-20.

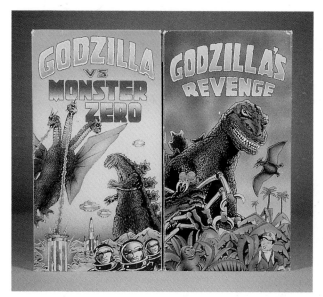

VI3014 and VI3008 *Godzilla's Revenge* and *Monster Zero* videos. Each $8-20.

Laserdiscs
Toho Video

VI4001	*Godzilla 1954* (TLL 2002, 2181 and 2182)	$50-80
VI4002	*Godzilla Raids Again* (TLL 2024 and 2204)	50-80
VI4003	*King Kong Vs. Godzilla* (TLL 2064 and 2183)	50-80
VI4004	*Godzilla vs. Mothra* (TLL 2021 and 2456)	50-80
VI4005	*Ghidrah, the Three Headed Monster* (TLL 2230)	50-80
VI4006	*Monster Zero* (TLL 2012, 2042 and 2233)	50-80
VI4007	*Godzilla vs. the Sea Monster* (TLL 2049 and 2231)	50-80
VI4008	*Son of Godzilla* (TLL 2077 and 2234)	50-80
VI4009	*Destroy All Monsters* (TLL 2058 and 2232)	50-80
VI4010	*Godzilla's Revenge* (TLL 2109 and 2484)	50-80
VI4011	*Godzilla vs. the Smog Monster* (TLL 2147 and 2485)	50-80
VI4012	*Godzilla vs. Gigan* (TLL 2228 and 2486)	50-80
VI4013	*Godzilla vs. Megalon* (TLL 2147 and 2487)	50-80
VI4014	*Godzilla vs. MechaGodzilla* (TLL 2086 and 2228)	50-80
VI4015	*Terror of MechaGodzilla* (TLL 2089 and 2229)	50-80
VI4016	*Godzilla 1984* (TLL 2027 and 2201)	50-80
VI4017	*Godzilla vs. Biollante* (TLL 2202, box set)	150-250
VI4117	*Godzilla vs. Biollante* (TLL 2174)	50-80
VI4018	*Godzilla vs. King Ghidora* (TLL 2389, box set)	150-250
VI4118	*Godzilla vs. King Ghidora* (2200)	50-80
VI4019	*Godzilla vs. Mothra 1992* (TLL 2434, box set)	150-250
VI4119	*Godzilla vs. Mothra 1992* (TLL 2453)	50-80
VI4020	*Godzilla vs. MechaGodzilla 1993* (TLL 2236, box set)	175-275
VI4120	*Godzilla vs. MechaGodzilla 1993* (TLL 2454)	50-80
VI4021	*Godzilla vs. SpaceGodzilla* (TLL 2276, box set)	140-200
VI4121	*Godzilla vs. SpaceGodzilla* (TLL 2455)	50-80
VI4022	*Godzilla vs. Destroyer* (TLL 2476, box set)	175-275
VI4201	*Godzilla Death Chronicles* Box set	250-400
VI4202	*Godzilla Fantasia/Legend of Godzilla* (TLL 2055)	80-140
VI4203	Godzilla 40th Anniversary Box set (TLL 2235)	150-225
VI4204	*Making of Godzilla (84)/Toho SFX Graffiti Vol. 1 & 2* (TLL 2038)	80-150
VI4205	*Symphonic Godzilla vs. MechaGodzilla* (TLL 2215)	40-60

US Laserdisc Releases

VI5001	*Godzilla King of the Monsters* (Vestron 3010)	$30-60
VI5002	*Godzilla, King of the Monsters* (Paramount)	20-40
VI5003	*Godzilla's Revenge* (Paramount)	20-40
VI5004	*Godzilla vs. the Smog Monster/Monster From a Prehistoric Planet* (Orion 6923)	50-80
VI5005	*Godzilla vs. Gigan/Godzilla vs. MechaGodzilla* (New World Video)	30-50
VI5006	*Terror of MechaGodzilla* (Paramount)	20-40
VI5007	*Godzilla 1985* (New World Video)	30-50
VI5008	*Godzilla vs. Biollante* (HBO-90838)	20-40

Left: VI4009 *Destroy All Monsters* Japanese laserdisc. $50-80.
Right: VI4002 *Godzilla Raids Again* Japanese laserdisc. $50-80.

VI4018 *Godzilla vs. King Ghidora*
Japanese laserdisc box set. $100-200.

VI4022 *Godzilla vs. Destroyer* Japanese
laserdisc box set. $175-275

VI5002 *Godzilla, King of the
Monsters* laserdisc. $20-40.

VI5004 *Godzilla vs. the Smog Monster* (w/*Monster
From a Prehistoric Planet*) laserdisc. $50-80.

Bibliography

Complete Collection of Godzilla. Tokyo, Japan: Kodansha, 1979.

Godzilla-Fantastic Collection No.5. Tokyo, Japan: Asahi Sonorama, 1978.

Godziszewski, Ed. *Illustrated Encyclopedia of Godzilla, The.* Manitoba, Canada: Daikaiju Enterprises, 1996.

Hobby Japan Extra, '93 Winter. Tokyo, Japan: Hobby Japan Pub., 1992

Hobby Japan Special Issue, Godzilla. Tokyo, Japan: Hobby Japan Pub., 1993

Hobby Japan Extra, '95 Winter. Tokyo, Japan: Hobby Japan Pub., 1994

Hobby Japan Extra, '96 Winter. Tokyo, Japan: Hobby Japan Pub., 1995

Kuraji, Takashi and Nishimura, Yuji. *Godzilla Toy Museum.* Tokyo, Japan: Bandai, 1992.

Nishimura, Yuji and Yamada, Masami. *Godzilla Museum.* Tokyo, Japan:

We Love Godzilla Everytime. Tokyo, Japan: Gakken, 1995.

Yamata, Seiji. *Godzilla Collection, Toho Special Effects Movie Poster Collection.* Tokyo, Japan: Data House, 1995.

Appendix

Resources

Conventions

There are two major conventions put on each year. Both come highly recommended and would be very enjoyable for any fan to attend. Contact the organizers at the addresses below for information.

Friends of G-Fan Magazine
Box 3468
Steinbach, Manitoba
Canada R0A 2A0

Kaiju-Con
c/o John Roberto
80 East 14th St. #4B
Brooklyn, NY 11230
(John also publishes Kaiju-Fan, a magazine that attempts to cover all Japanese fantastic cinema)

Dealers

We have listed a few dealers below, not only because of their expertise and experience in the field, but also as they were helpful to us in the preparation of this book. This is by no means a complete list of all the dealers in Godzilla merchandise. With a little detective work, you will be able to locate other dealers with excellent reputations and quality items waiting to be of service.

Club Daikaiju
P.O.Box 1614
Fort Lee, NJ 07024

Creature Feature Productions
P.O. Box 6438
Boston, MA 02114

Showcase Collectibles
4470 Chamblee Dunwoody Rd. Suite 451
Atlanta, GA 30338

Publications

Here are also a few of the publications worthy of mention that focus solely on Godzilla and other Japanese monsters. They have ads from dealers as well as the newest information on movies and products.

G-Fan Magazine
c/o Daikaiju Enterprises
Box 3468
Steinbach, Manitoba
Canada R0A 2A0

Japanese Giants
P.O. Box 357
Wilmette, IL 60091

Monster Attack Team
13352 Maham #282
Dallas, TX 75240-6121

And finally no "where to buy and sell list" would be complete without mentioning the premiere magazines for collectors of toys and movie posters in general. Each is published twice a month and is full of ads from dealers all over the world. Both magazines are essential for collectors of all types. Write or call each of these publishers for a sample copy.

Movie Collector's World
c/o Arena Publishing
P.O.Box 309
Fraser, MI 48066
810-774-4311

Toy Shop
c/o Krause Publications
700 E. State St.
Iola, WI 54990
(715) 445-2214